THE ADVENTURES OF
TONY MILLIONAIRE'S SOCK MONKEY

For Mildred,
who gave me my
first sock monkey

Editor
PHILIP D. AMARA

Book Design
CARY GRAZZINI

Publisher
MIKE RICHARDSON

THE ADVENTURES OF TONY MILLIONAIRE'S SOCK MONKEY™

This book collects Volume One, issues #1-2, and Volume Two, issues #1-2,
of the Dark Horse comic-book series *Sock Monkey*™.

Published by
Dark Horse Comics, Inc.
10956 SE Main Street
Milwaukie, OR 97222

First edition: July 2000
ISBN: 1-56971-490-8

1 3 5 7 9 10 8 6 4 2

PRINTED IN CANADA

The Adventures of
SOCK MONKEY™

by
TONY MILLIONAIRE

Introduction by
JOHN FLANSBURGH

INTRODUCTION

 MET TONY MILLIONAIRE IN Williamsburgh, Brooklyn around 1990. He was living locally and contributing a comic strip with what seemed like an ever-changing title, but I believe was officially called "Medea's Weekend," to a neighborhood newsletter, the *Waterfront Week*. It was a four-page Xeroxed periodical that was too far ahead of its time. Well-drawn and graphically sophisticated, Millionaire's strip was fascinating to me in that it openly ignored standard strip "punchlines" in the larger panels, usually opting instead for a brutal suicide or murder to finish off the final panel. Then, in a simplified mini-strip that often ran along the border, Millionaire would slip in a hilarious two-line joke that was funnier than most syndicated comics on their best day.

Williamsburgh was hardly a village, but its isolation from Manhattan and lower Brooklyn did create a tighter creative community than your average New York neighborhood. Word of Tony Millionaire's revelling became local legend. When I finally met the man in the briefest of exchanges, he was stomping down the street on his way to a bar with our mutual friends as I was on my way to my studio. He was very, very tall and physically imposing. Moments after our introduction, with just the slightest prompting, Tony had pulled some false teeth out of his head and was talking loudly about how his fighting days were behind him. I took his word for it, and we parted. Over the next couple of years he would do a number of illustrations for my band They Might Be Giants, including the cover of the CD *Then: The Earlier Years*, and he earned himself a spot in the scrappy upstart culture paper, the *New York Press*.

His new strip, entitled "Maakies," was clearly a hit and became a feature in dozens of culture weeklies around the US. Ultimately, Tony's work would expand to include magazine and book illustration, some animated "Maakies" for *Saturday Night Live*, and a series of *Sock Monkey* adventures, first published as a series, and now compiled here.

As his work has developed, both Millionaire's graphic line and enigmatic storytelling sensibility have come to remind me of one of the first and finest newspaper comic strips, *Little Nemo in Slumberland*. Like *Little Nemo*, Millionaire creates his own universe within a real-world setting, often incorporating historical architectural elements. We see his familiar domestic landscapes in stillness. These pastoral backdrops are a stage for Millionaire's adventures in pure imagination. The stories, distorted through the lens found at the bottom of an empty whiskey glass, are as manic as the settings are dignified. It's hard to sum up why these strips work so well, especially with their often violent crash endings, but I suspect they remind us of our own play as children: the bed is the sea, and everybody dies at the end, but they'll be back later.

— John Flansburgh
Williamsburgh, Brooklyn

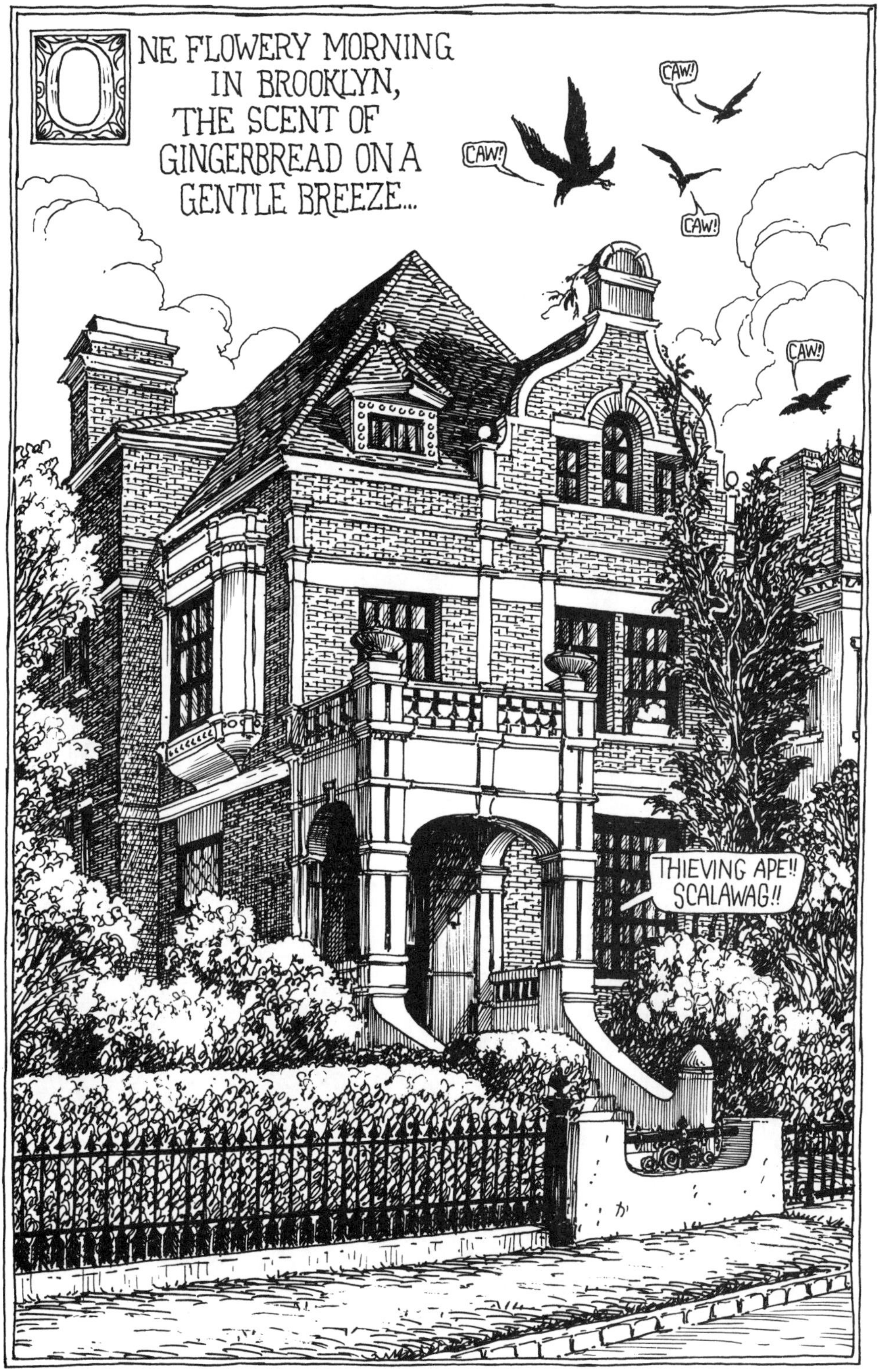
ONE FLOWERY MORNING IN BROOKLYN, THE SCENT OF GINGERBREAD ON A GENTLE BREEZE...
CAW!
CAW!
CAW!
CAW!
THIEVING APE!! SCALAWAG!!

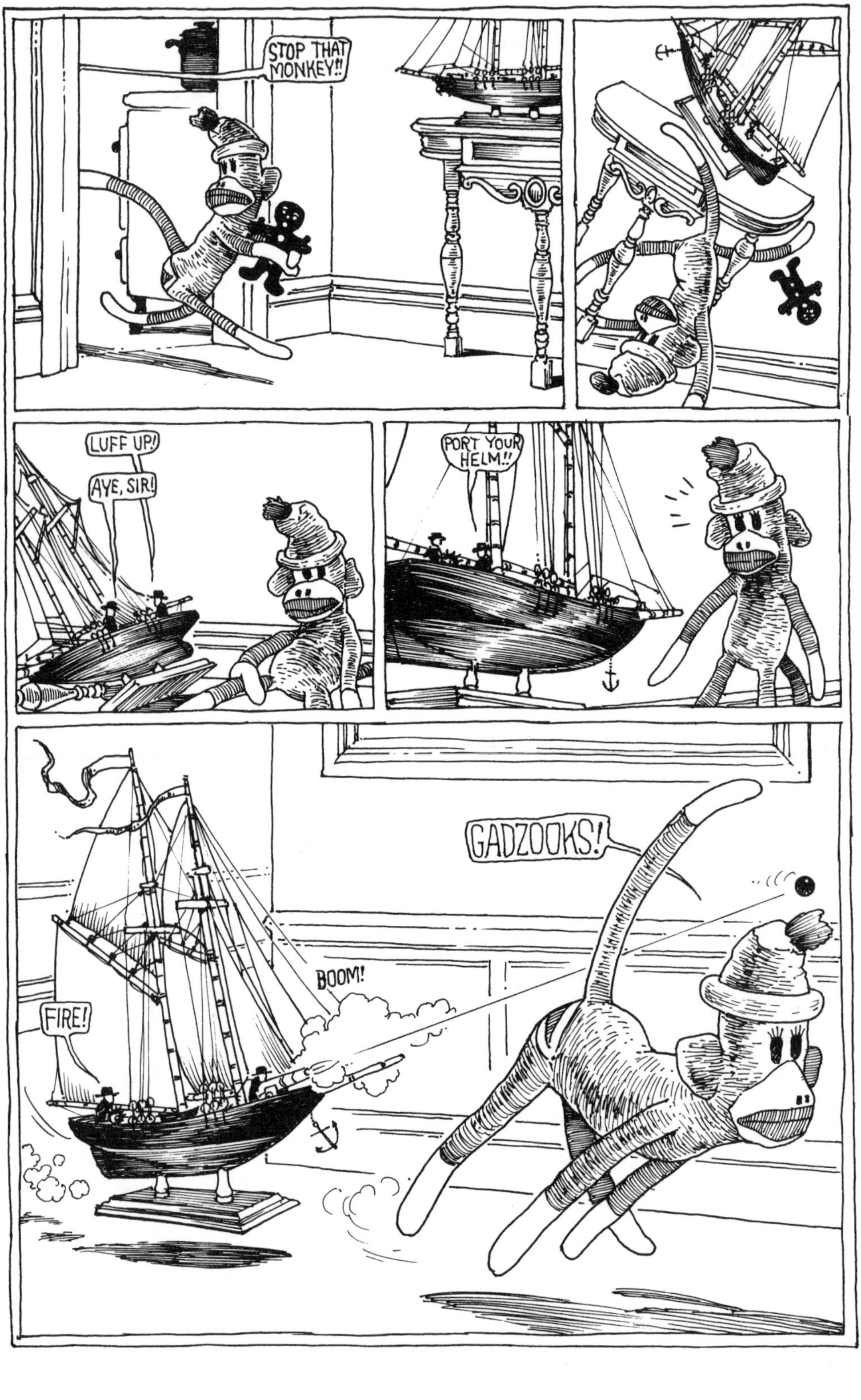
STOP THAT MONKEY!!
LUFF UP!
AYE, SIR!
PORT YOUR HELM!!
GADZOOKS!
BOOM!
FIRE!

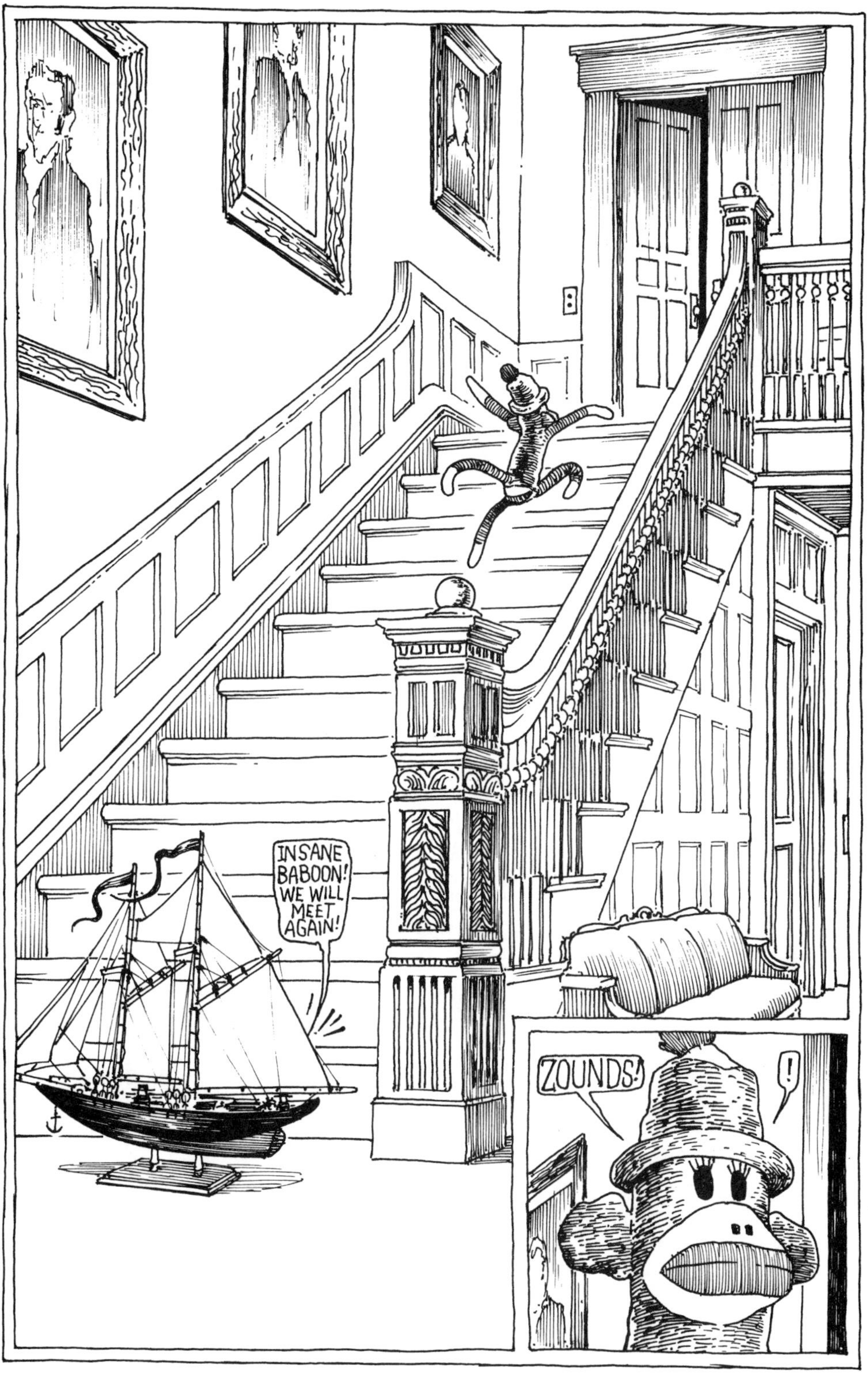
INSANE BABOON! WE WILL MEET AGAIN!
ZOUNDS!
!

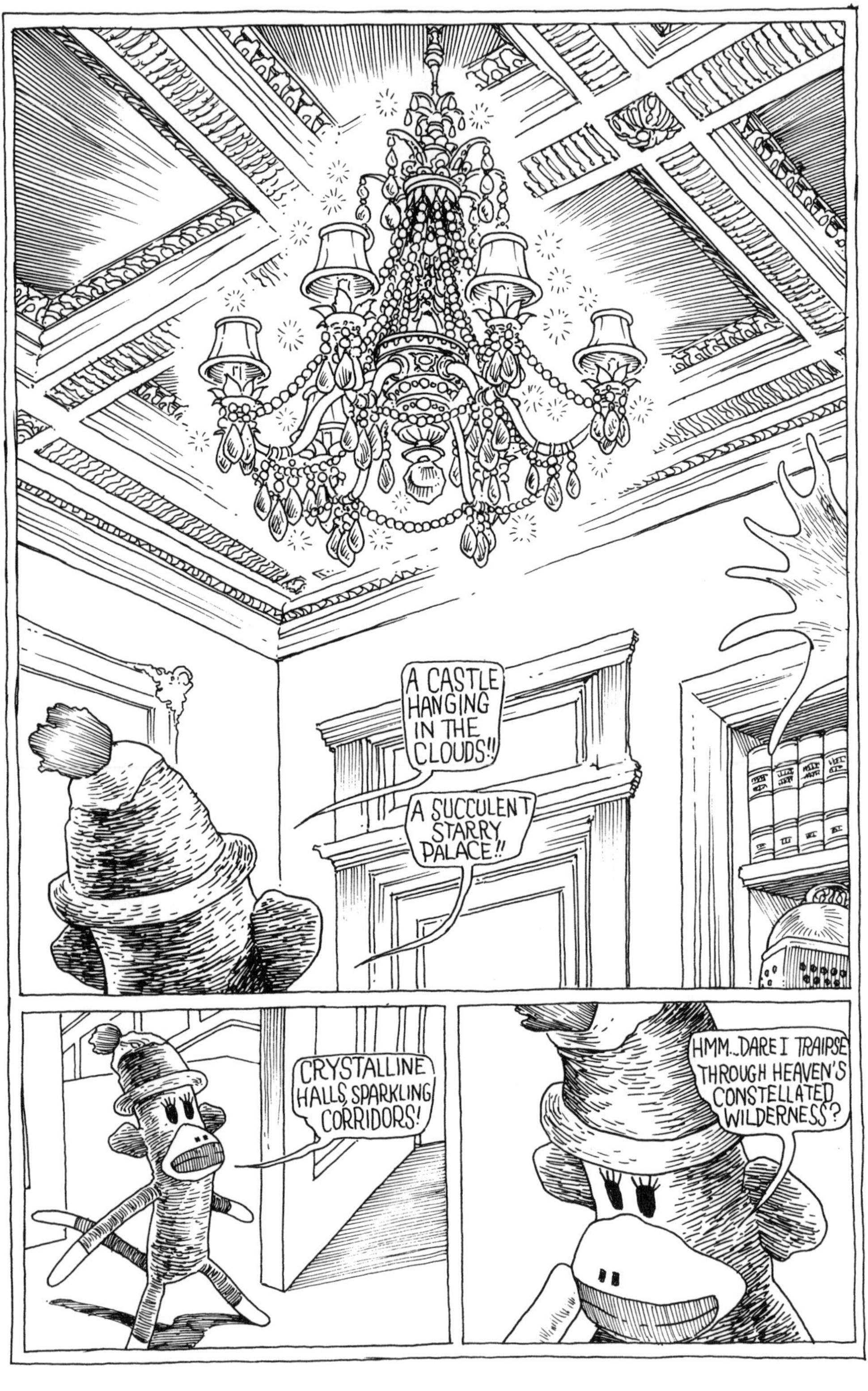
A CASTLE HANGING IN THE CLOUDS!!
A SUCCULENT STARRY PALACE!!
CRYSTALLINE HALLS, SPARKLING CORRIDORS!
HMM...DARE I TRAIPSE THROUGH HEAVEN'S CONSTELLATED WILDERNESS?

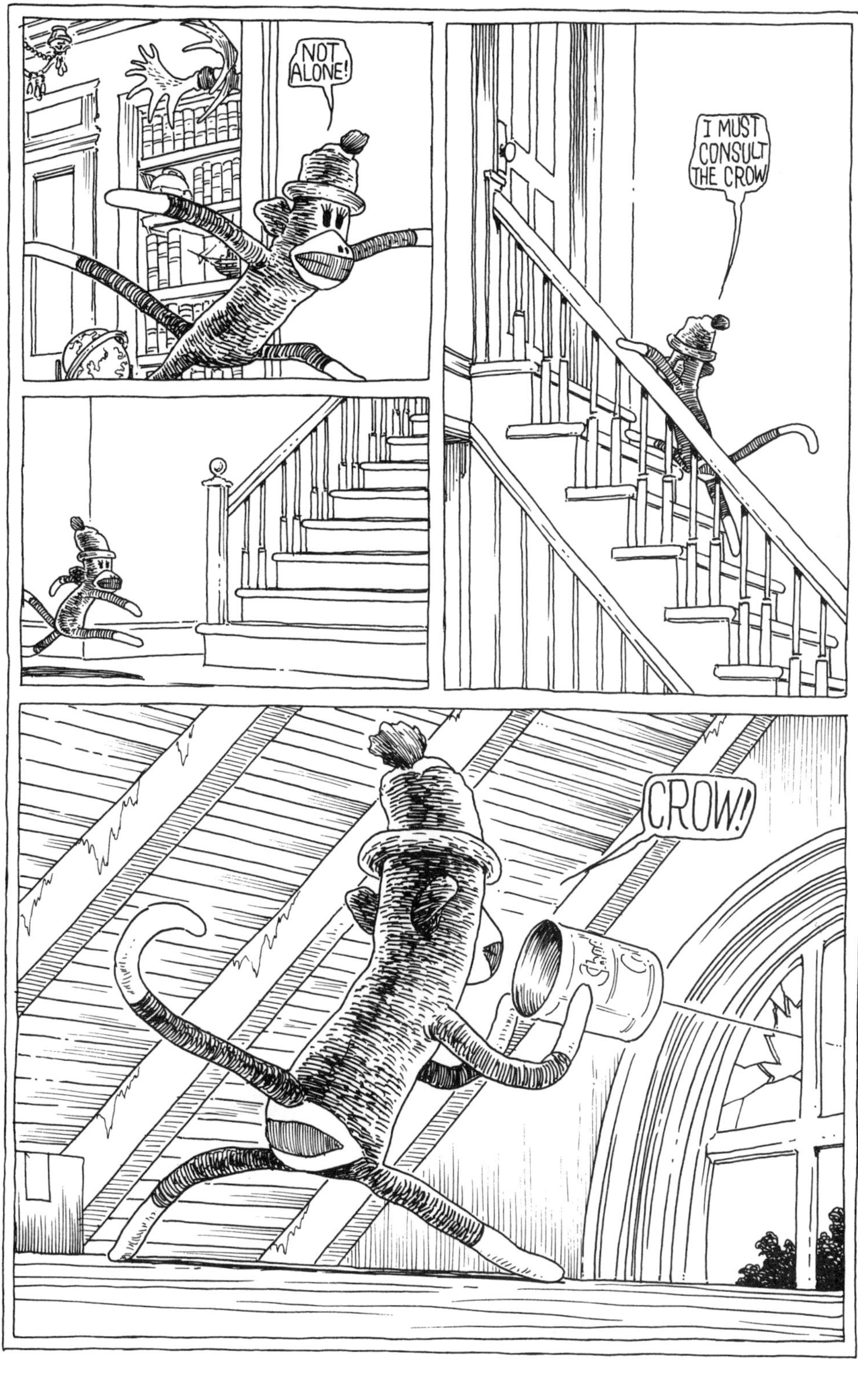
NOT ALONE!
I MUST CONSULT THE CROW
CROW!

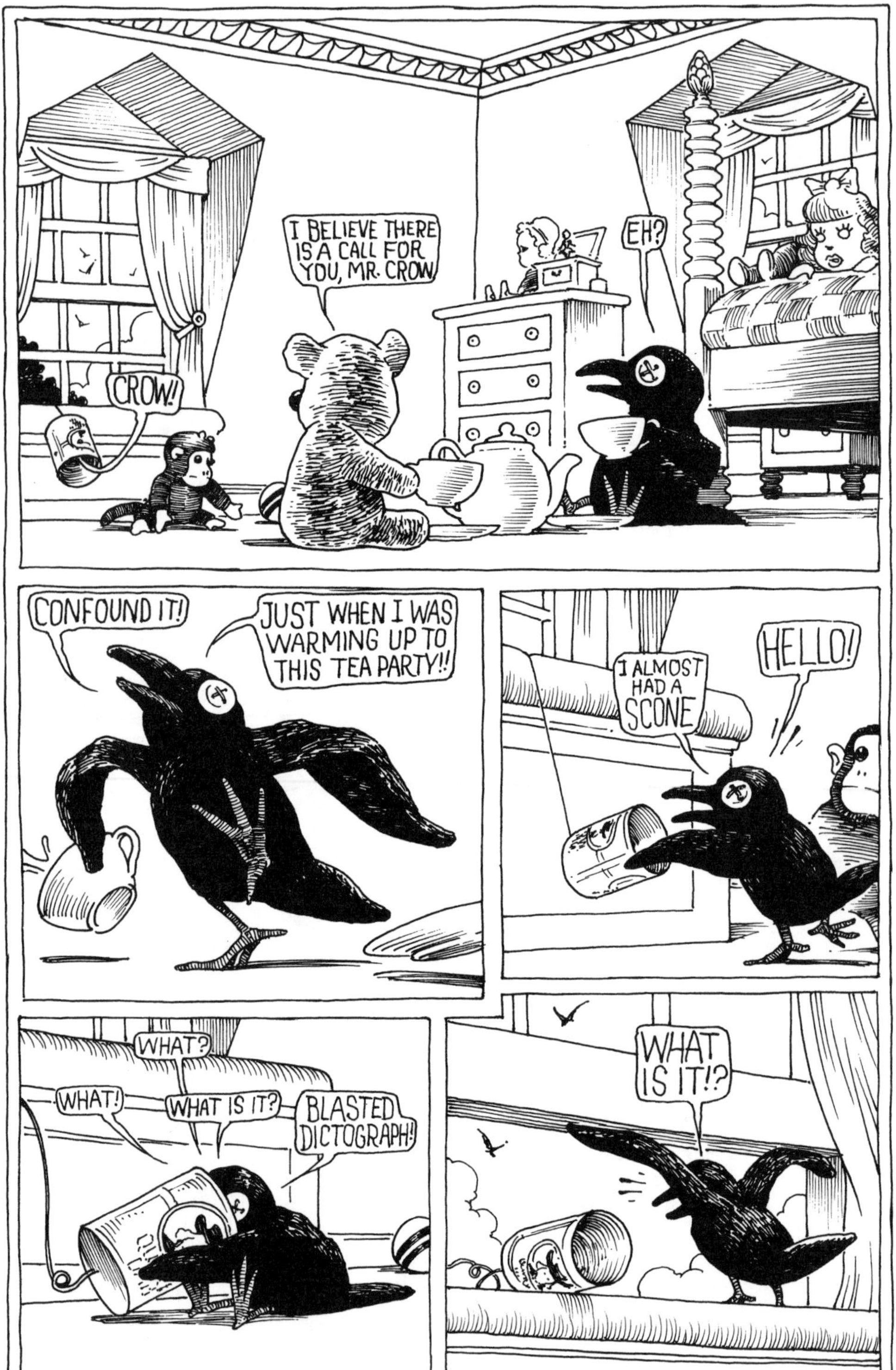
I BELIEVE THERE IS A CALL FOR YOU, MR. CROW
EH?
CROW!
CONFOUND IT!
JUST WHEN I WAS WARMING UP TO THIS TEA PARTY!!
HELLO!
I ALMOST HAD A SCONE
WHAT?
WHAT!
WHAT IS IT?
BLASTED DICTOGRAPH!
WHAT IS IT!?

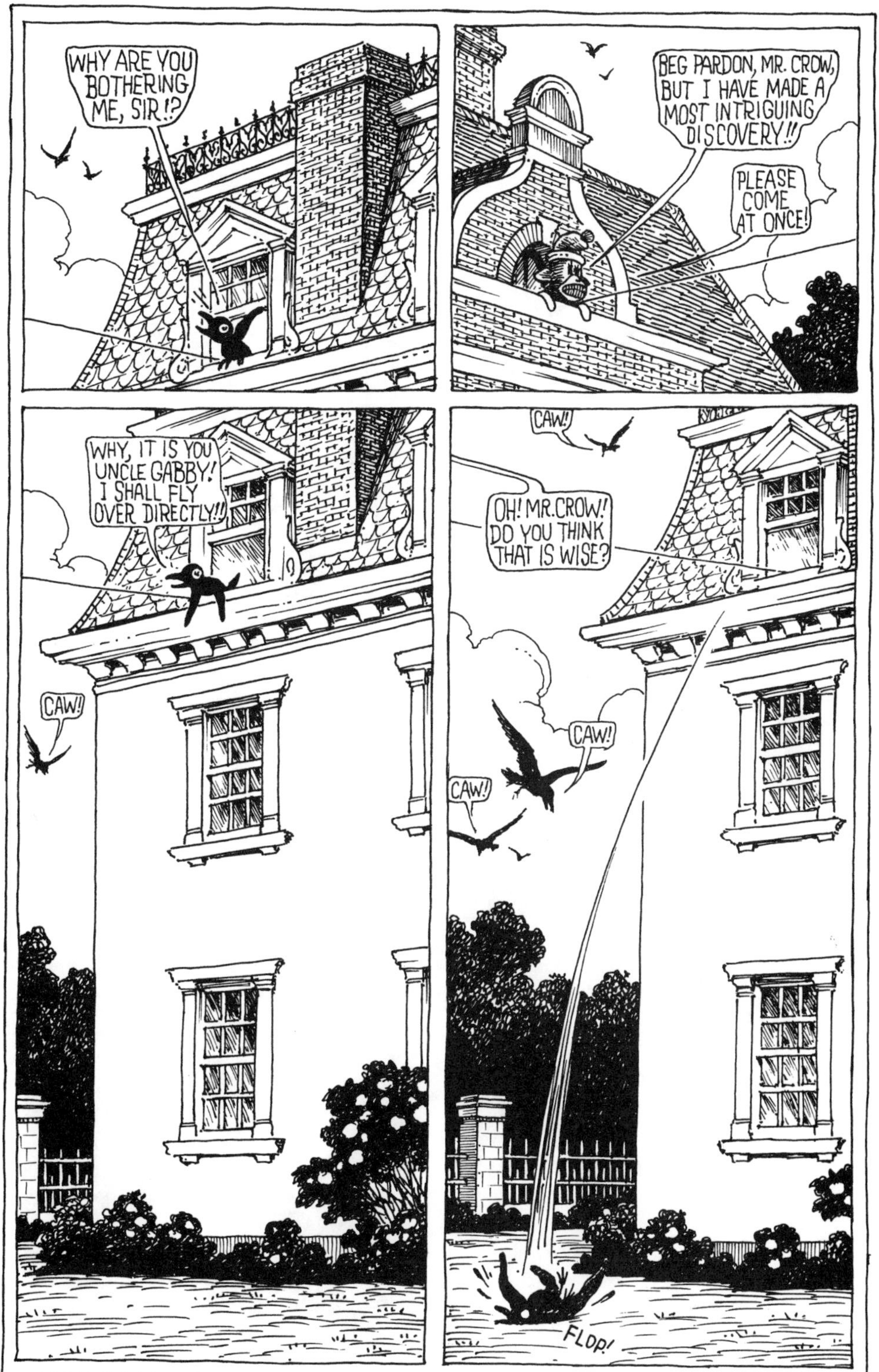
WHY ARE YOU BOTHERING ME, SIR!?
BEG PARDON, MR. CROW, BUT I HAVE MADE A MOST INTRIGUING DISCOVERY!!
PLEASE COME AT ONCE!
WHY, IT IS YOU UNCLE GABBY! I SHALL FLY OVER DIRECTLY!!
CAW!
CAW!
OH! MR. CROW! DO YOU THINK THAT IS WISE?
CAW!
CAW!
FLOP!

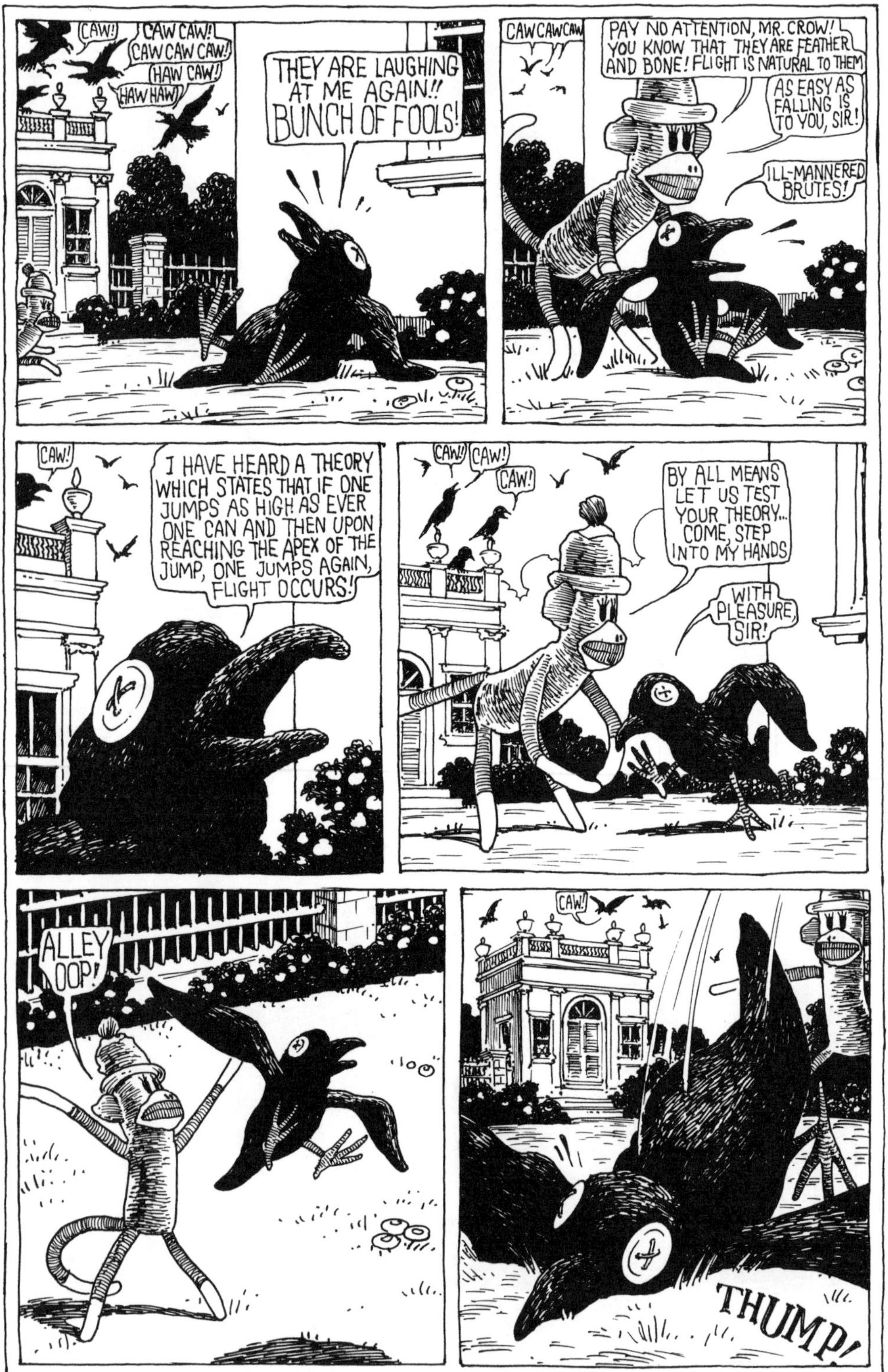
CAW!
CAW CAW! CAW CAW CAW!
HAW CAW!
HAW HAW!
THEY ARE LAUGHING AT ME AGAIN!! BUNCH OF FOOLS!
CAW CAW CAW
PAY NO ATTENTION, MR. CROW! YOU KNOW THAT THEY ARE FEATHER AND BONE! FLIGHT IS NATURAL TO THEM
AS EASY AS FALLING IS TO YOU, SIR!
ILL-MANNERED BRUTES!
CAW!
I HAVE HEARD A THEORY WHICH STATES THAT IF ONE JUMPS AS HIGH AS EVER ONE CAN AND THEN UPON REACHING THE APEX OF THE JUMP, ONE JUMPS AGAIN, FLIGHT OCCURS!
CAW! CAW!
CAW!
BY ALL MEANS LET US TEST YOUR THEORY... COME, STEP INTO MY HANDS
WITH PLEASURE, SIR!
ALLEY OOP!
CAW!
THUMP!

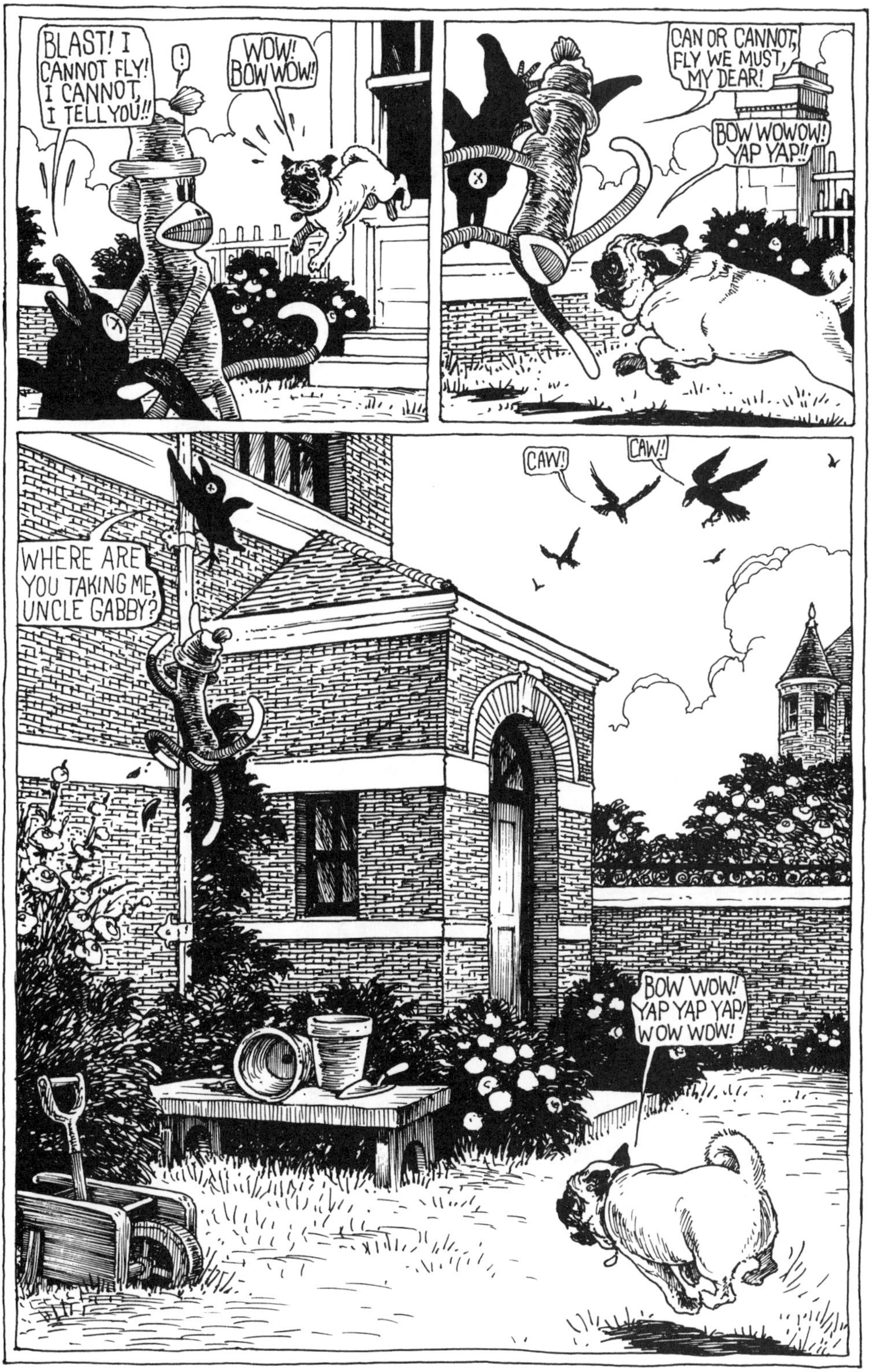
BLAST! I CANNOT FLY! I CANNOT, I TELL YOU!!
!
WOW! BOW WOW!
CAN OR CANNOT, FLY WE MUST, MY DEAR!
BOW WOWOW! YAP YAP!!
WHERE ARE YOU TAKING ME, UNCLE GABBY?
CAW!
CAW!
BOW WOW! YAP YAP YAP! WOW WOW!

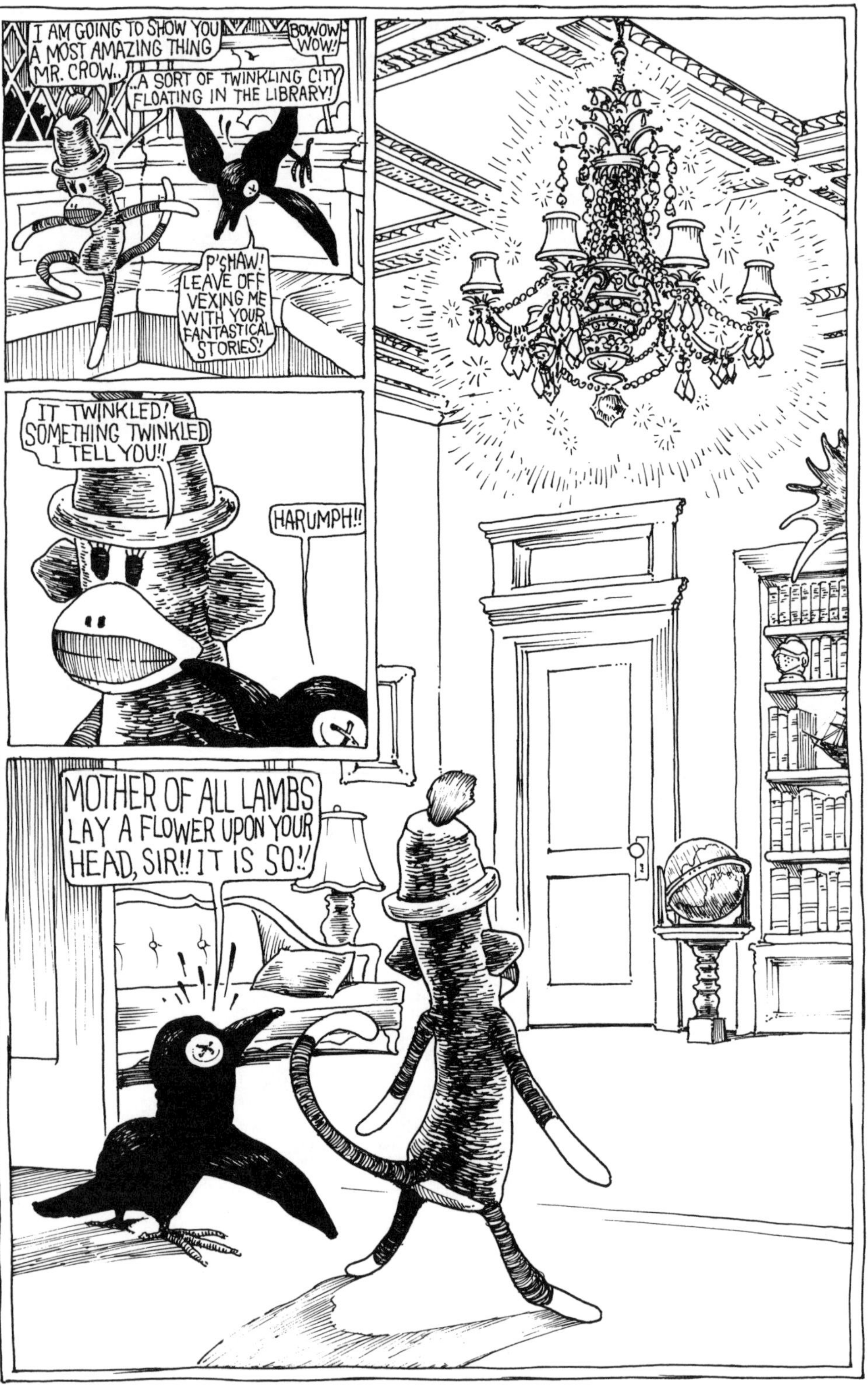
I AM GOING TO SHOW YOU A MOST AMAZING THING MR. CROW..
BOWOW WOW!
..A SORT OF TWINKLING CITY FLOATING IN THE LIBRARY!
P'SHAW! LEAVE OFF VEXING ME WITH YOUR FANTASTICAL STORIES!
IT TWINKLED! SOMETHING TWINKLED I TELL YOU!!
HARUMPH!!
MOTHER OF ALL LAMBS LAY A FLOWER UPON YOUR HEAD, SIR!! IT IS SO!!

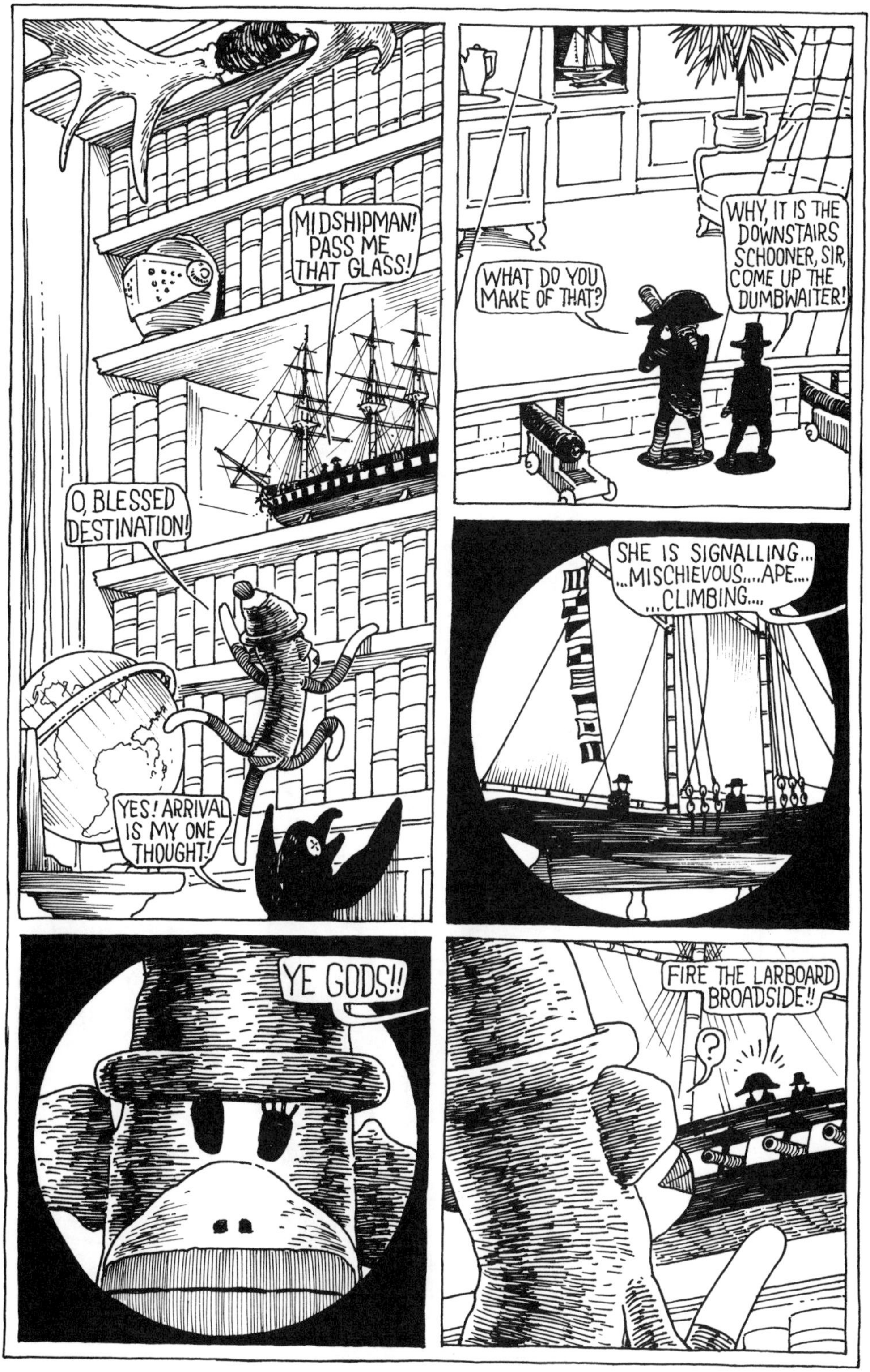
MIDSHIPMAN! PASS ME THAT GLASS!
O, BLESSED DESTINATION!
YES! ARRIVAL IS MY ONE THOUGHT!
WHAT DO YOU MAKE OF THAT?
WHY, IT IS THE DOWNSTAIRS SCHOONER, SIR, COME UP THE DUMBWAITER!
SHE IS SIGNALLING... ...MISCHIEVOUS.....APE.... ...CLIMBING....
YE GODS!!
FIRE THE LARBOARD BROADSIDE!!
?

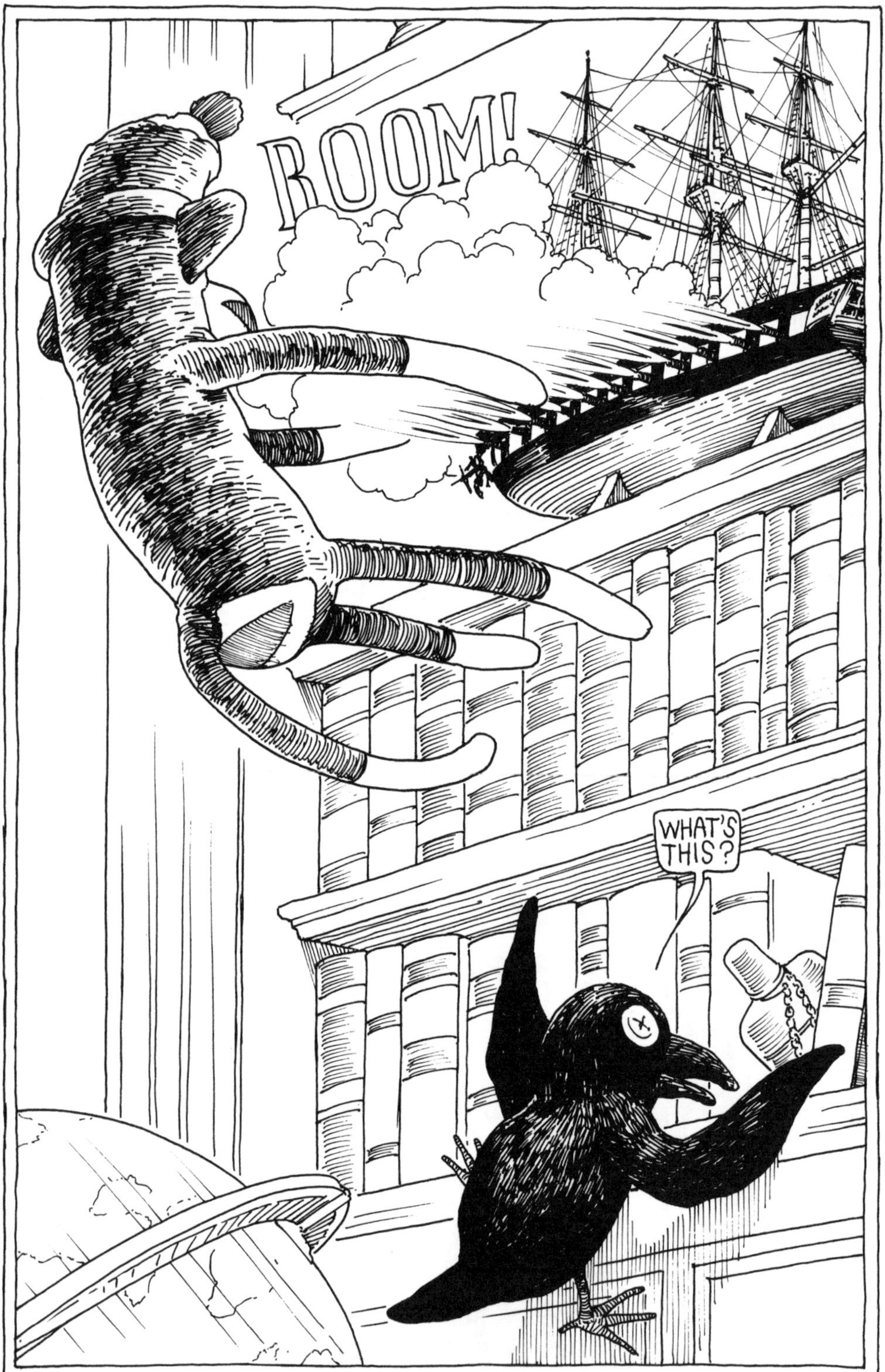
BOOM!
WHAT'S THIS?

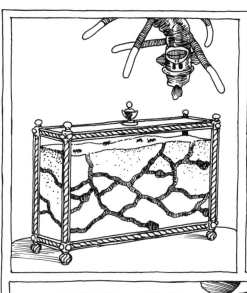

ONE THOUSAND PARDONS, SAHIB, I HAVE RUINED YOUR GLASSY DESERT!

ON THE CONTRARY, SIR! YOU HAVE RESCUED US!

RESCUED!? HOW IS THAT?

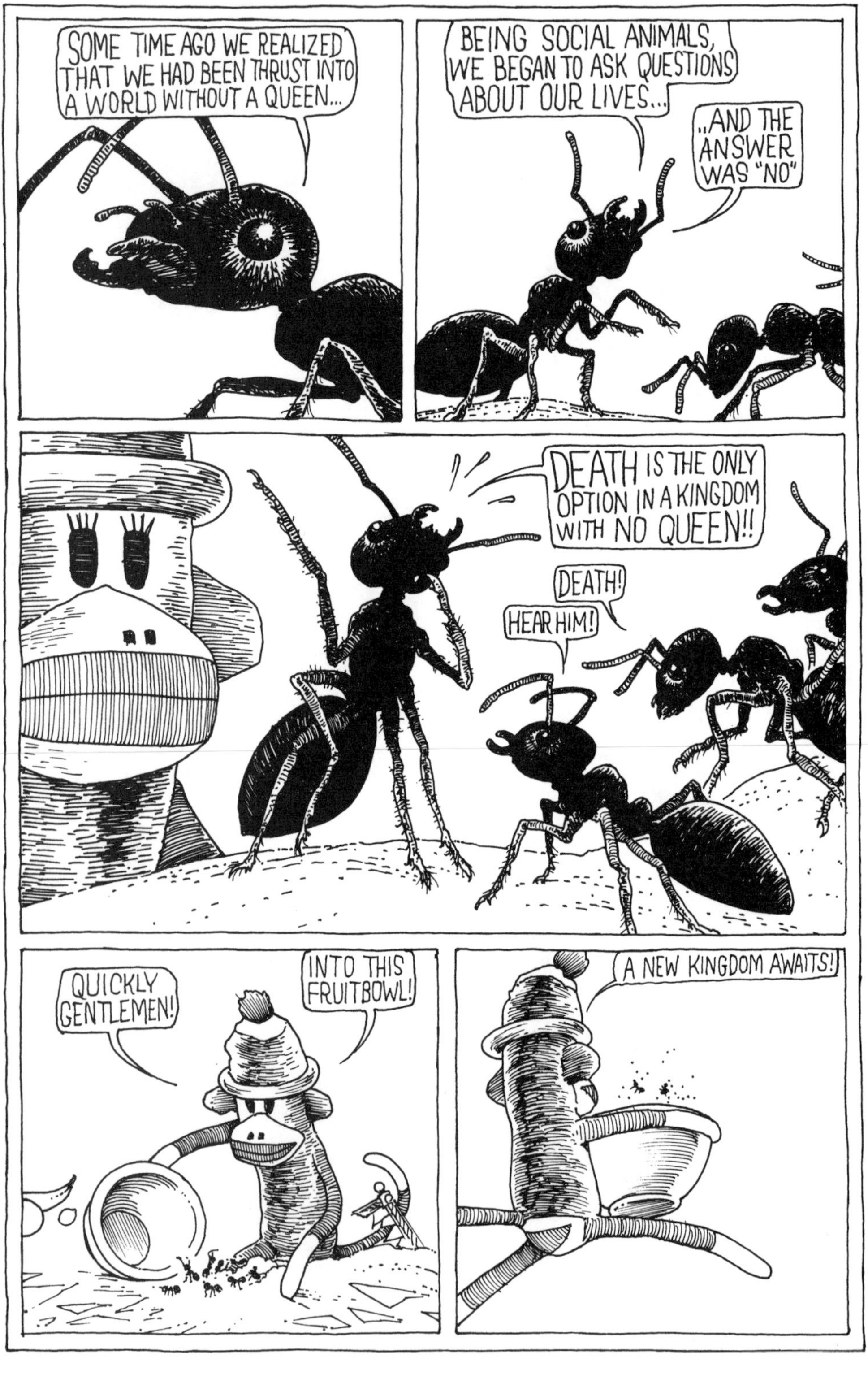
SOME TIME AGO WE REALIZED THAT WE HAD BEEN THRUST INTO A WORLD WITHOUT A QUEEN...
BEING SOCIAL ANIMALS, WE BEGAN TO ASK QUESTIONS ABOUT OUR LIVES...
..AND THE ANSWER WAS "NO"
DEATH IS THE ONLY OPTION IN A KINGDOM WITH NO QUEEN!!
DEATH!
HEAR HIM!
QUICKLY GENTLEMEN!
INTO THIS FRUITBOWL!
A NEW KINGDOM AWAITS!

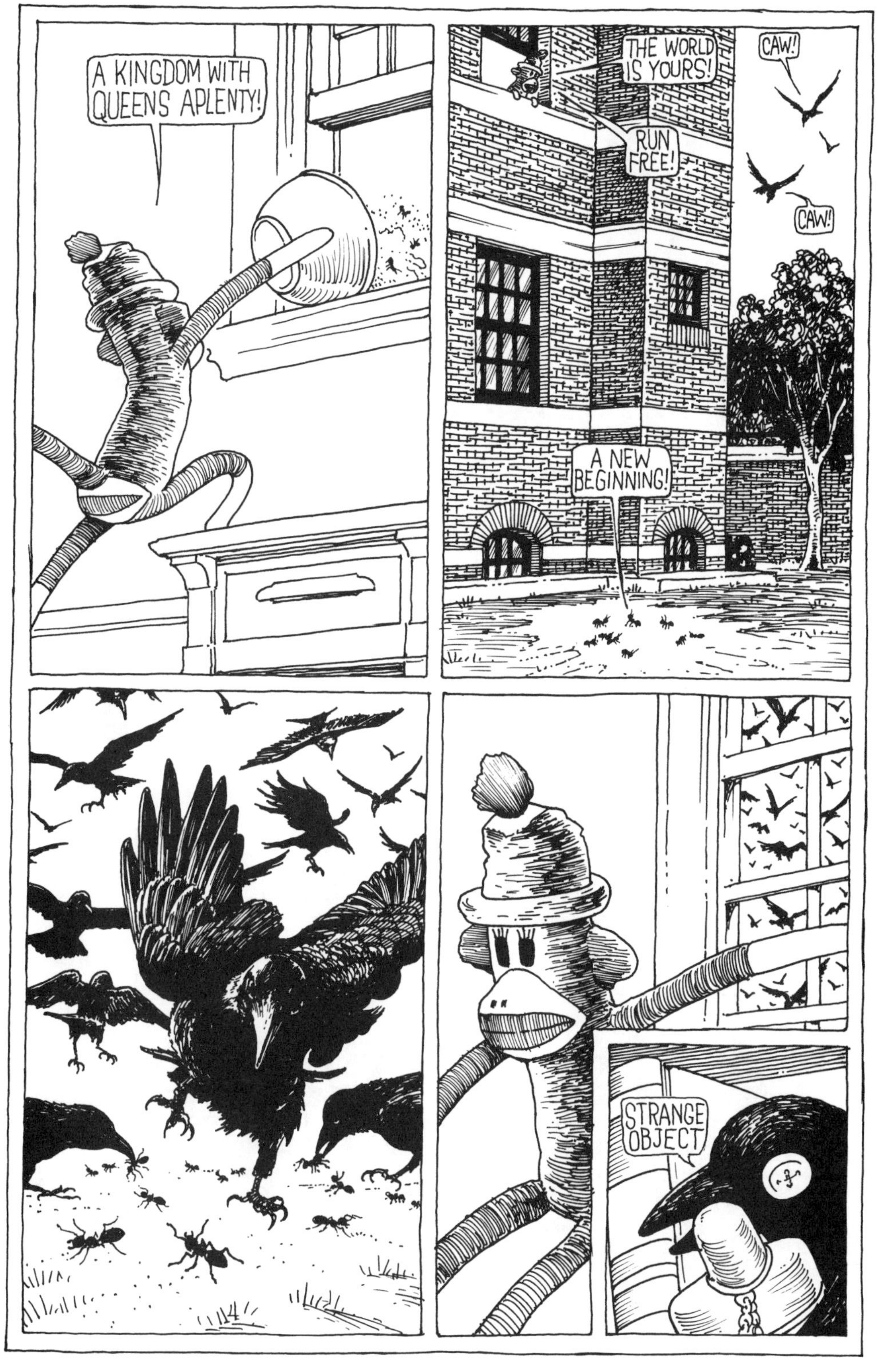
A KINGDOM WITH QUEENS APLENTY!
THE WORLD IS YOURS!
RUN FREE!
CAW!
CAW!
A NEW BEGINNING!
STRANGE OBJECT

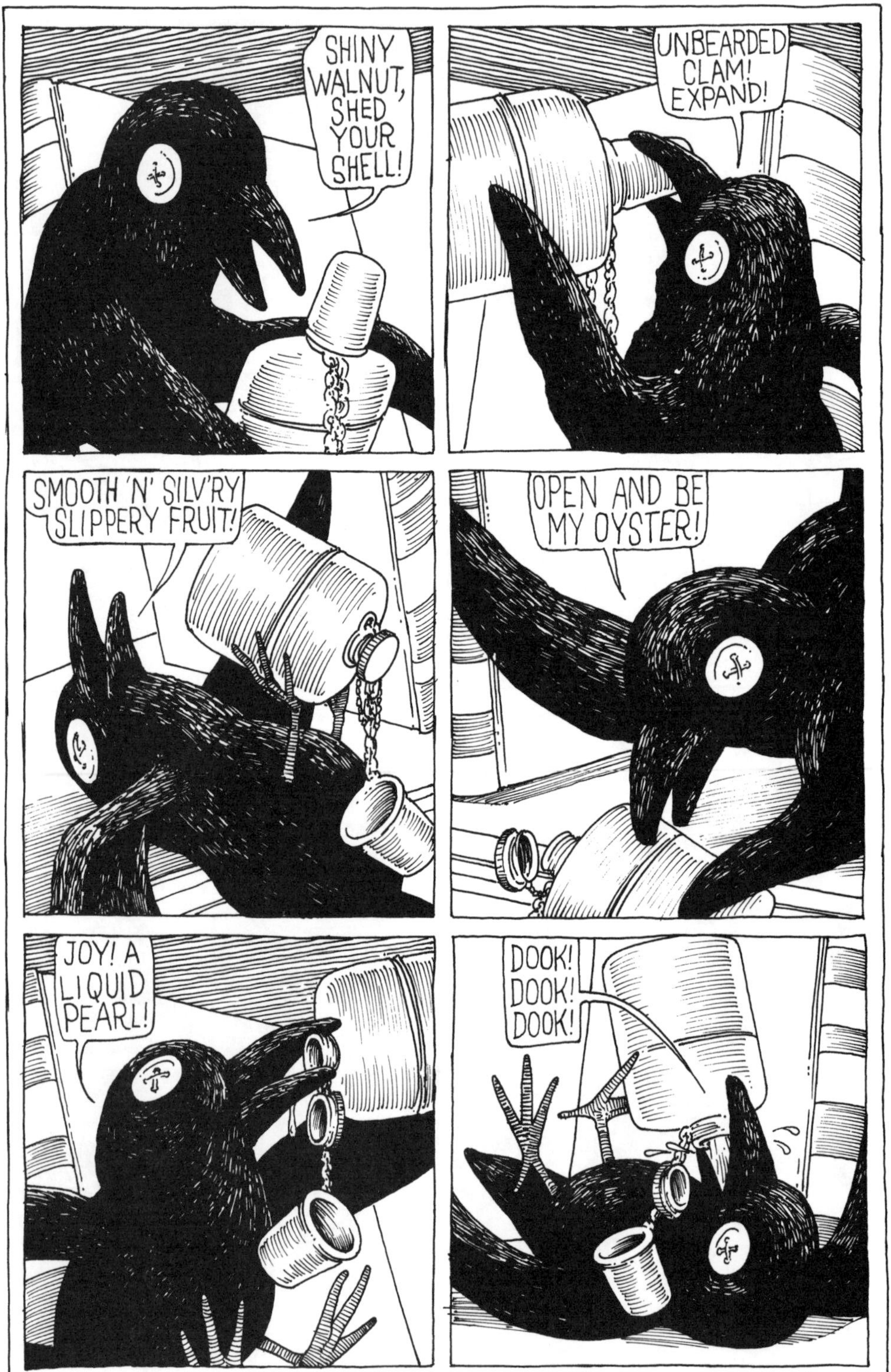
SHINY WALNUT, SHED YOUR SHELL!
UNBEARDED CLAM! EXPAND!
SMOOTH 'N' SILV'RY SLIPPERY FRUIT!
OPEN AND BE MY OYSTER!
JOY! A LIQUID PEARL!
DOOK! DOOK! DOOK!

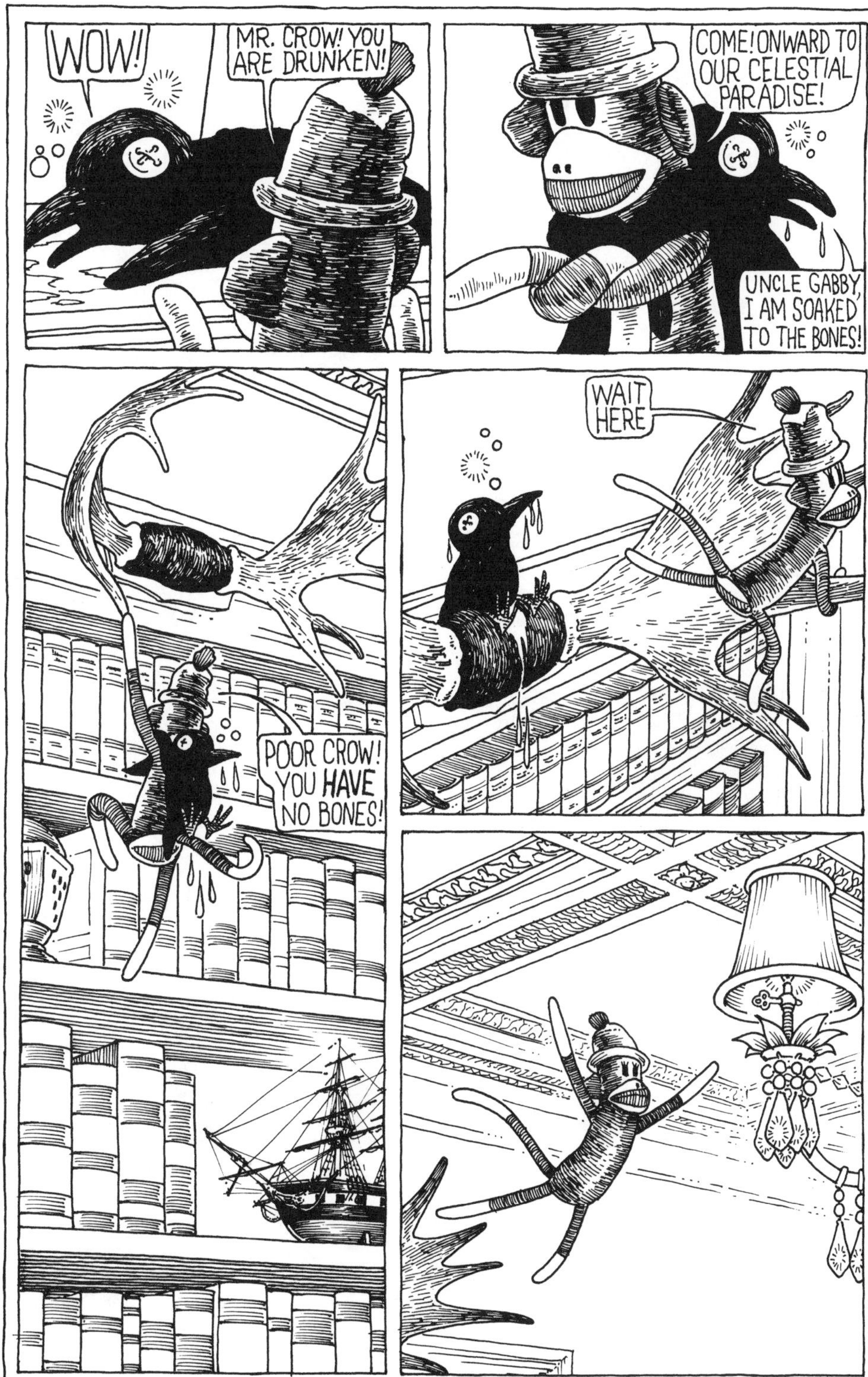
WOW!
MR. CROW! YOU ARE DRUNKEN!
COME! ONWARD TO OUR CELESTIAL PARADISE!
UNCLE GABBY, I AM SOAKED TO THE BONES!
POOR CROW! YOU HAVE NO BONES!
WAIT HERE

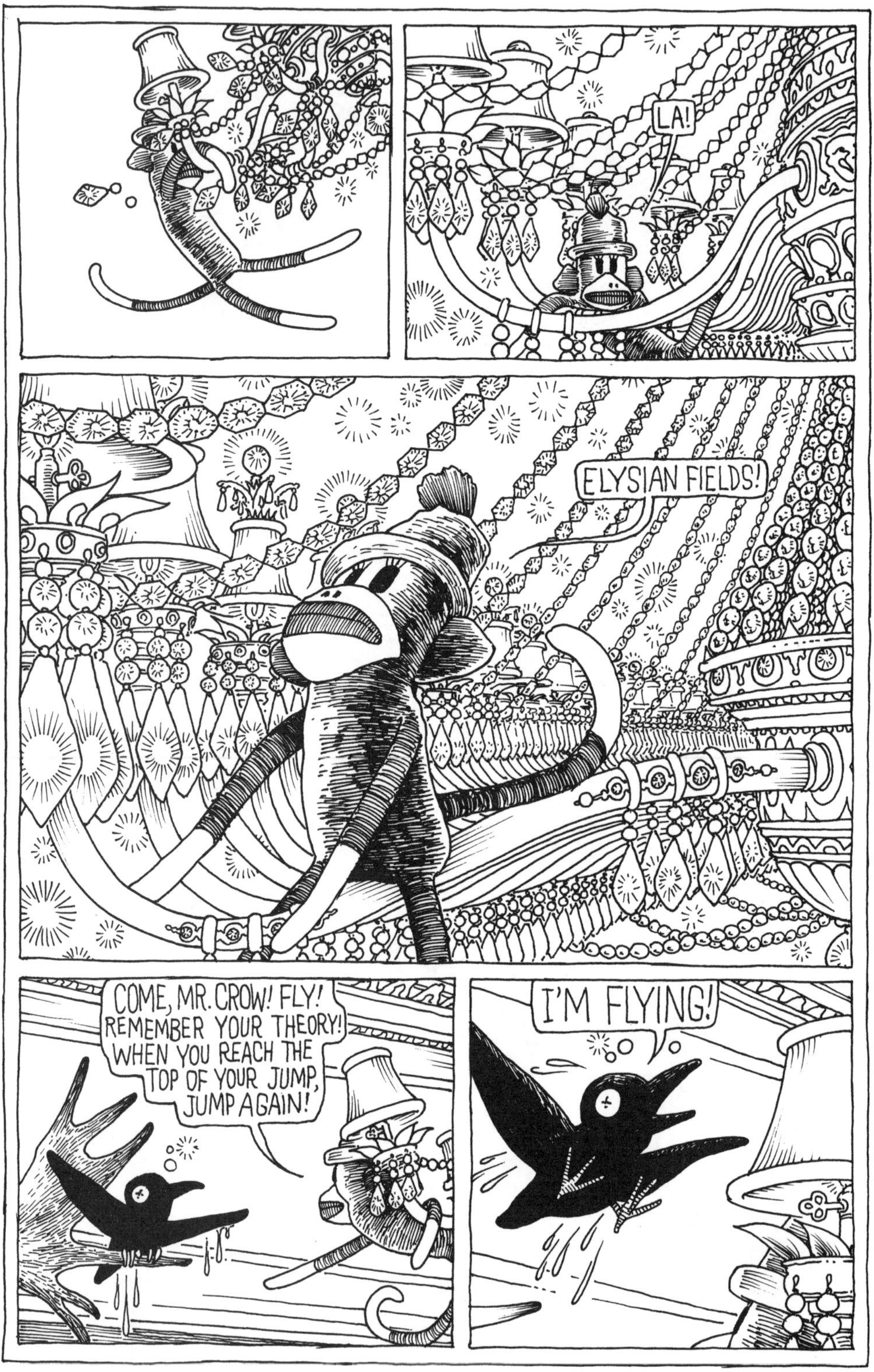
LA!
ELYSIAN FIELDS!
COME, MR. CROW! FLY! REMEMBER YOUR THEORY! WHEN YOU REACH THE TOP OF YOUR JUMP, JUMP AGAIN!
I'M FLYING!

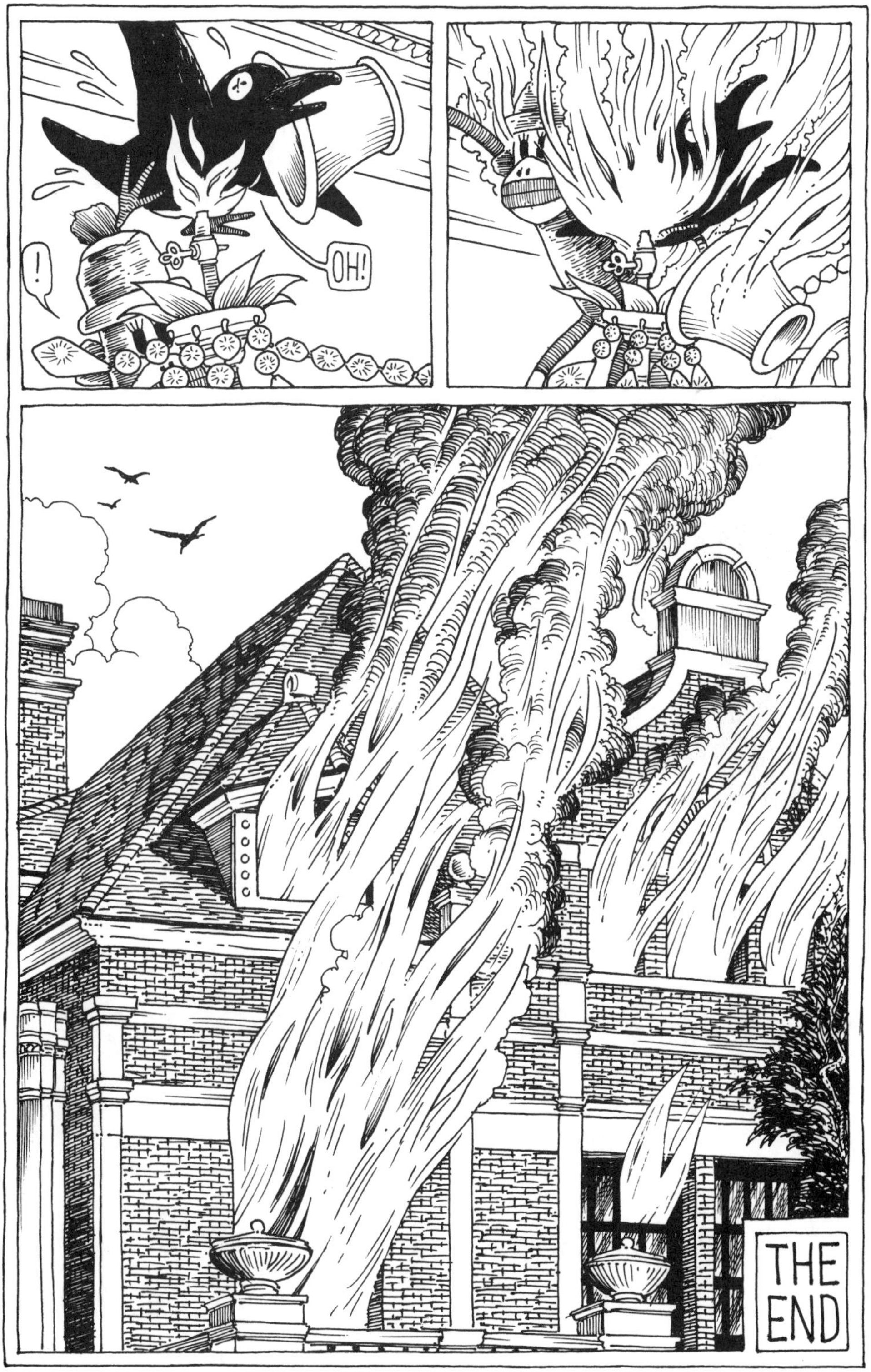
!
OH!
THE END

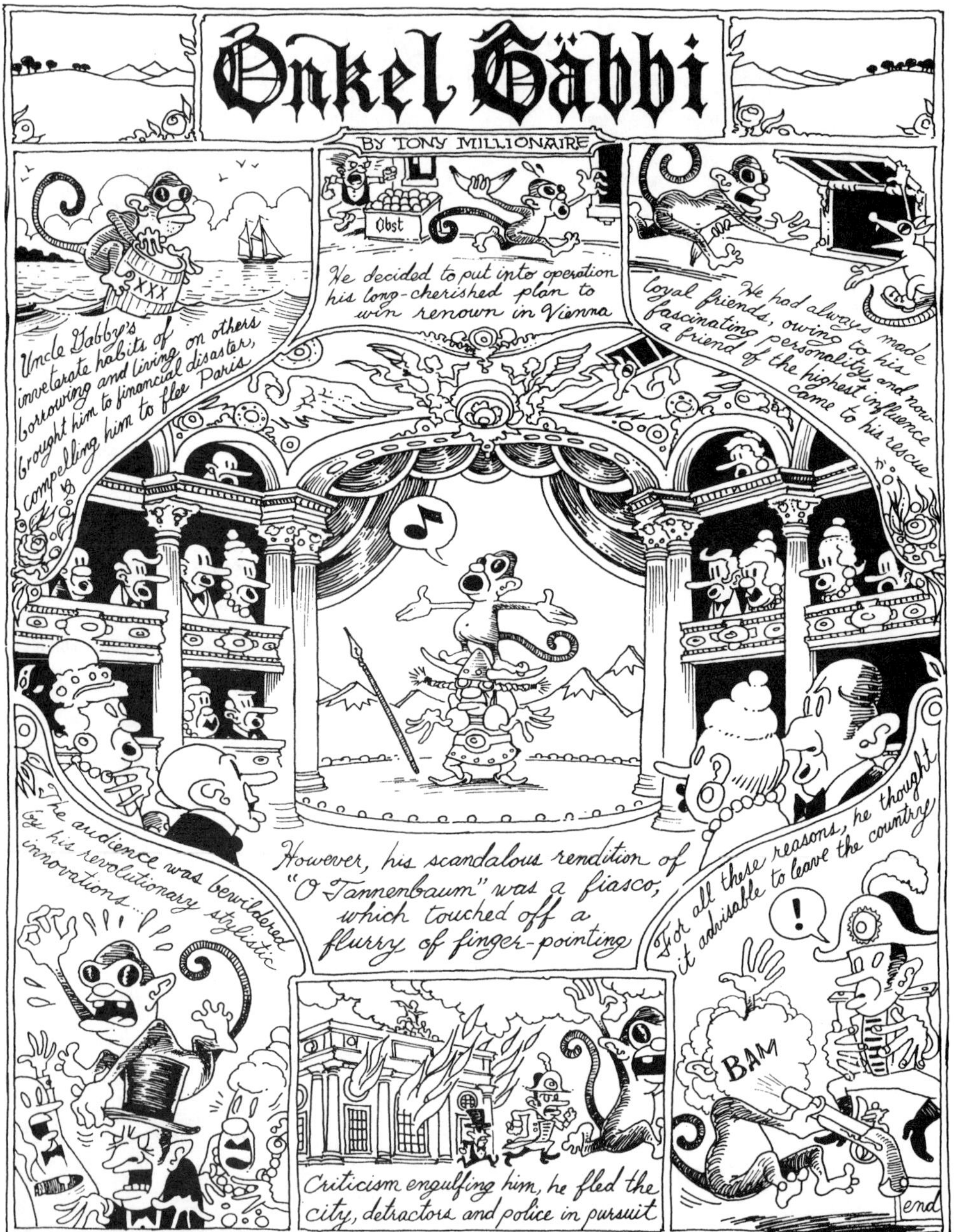
Onkel Gäbbi
BY TONY MILLIONAIRE
XXX
Uncle Gabby's inveterate habits of borrowing and living on others brought him to financial disaster, compelling him to flee Paris
Obst
He decided to put into operation his long-cherished plan to win renown in Vienna
He had always made loyal friends, owing to his fascinating personality, and now a friend of the highest influence came to his rescue
The audience was bewildered by his revolutionary stylistic innovations...
However, his scandalous rendition of "O Tannenbaum" was a fiasco, which touched off a flurry of finger-pointing
For all these reasons, he thought it advisable to leave the country
!
Criticism engulfing him, he fled the city, detractors and police in pursuit
BAM
end

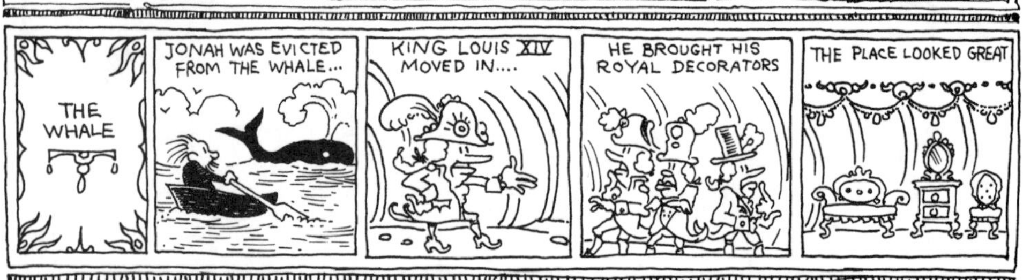
THE WHALE
JONAH WAS EVICTED FROM THE WHALE...
KING LOUIS XIV MOVED IN....
HE BROUGHT HIS ROYAL DECORATORS
THE PLACE LOOKED GREAT

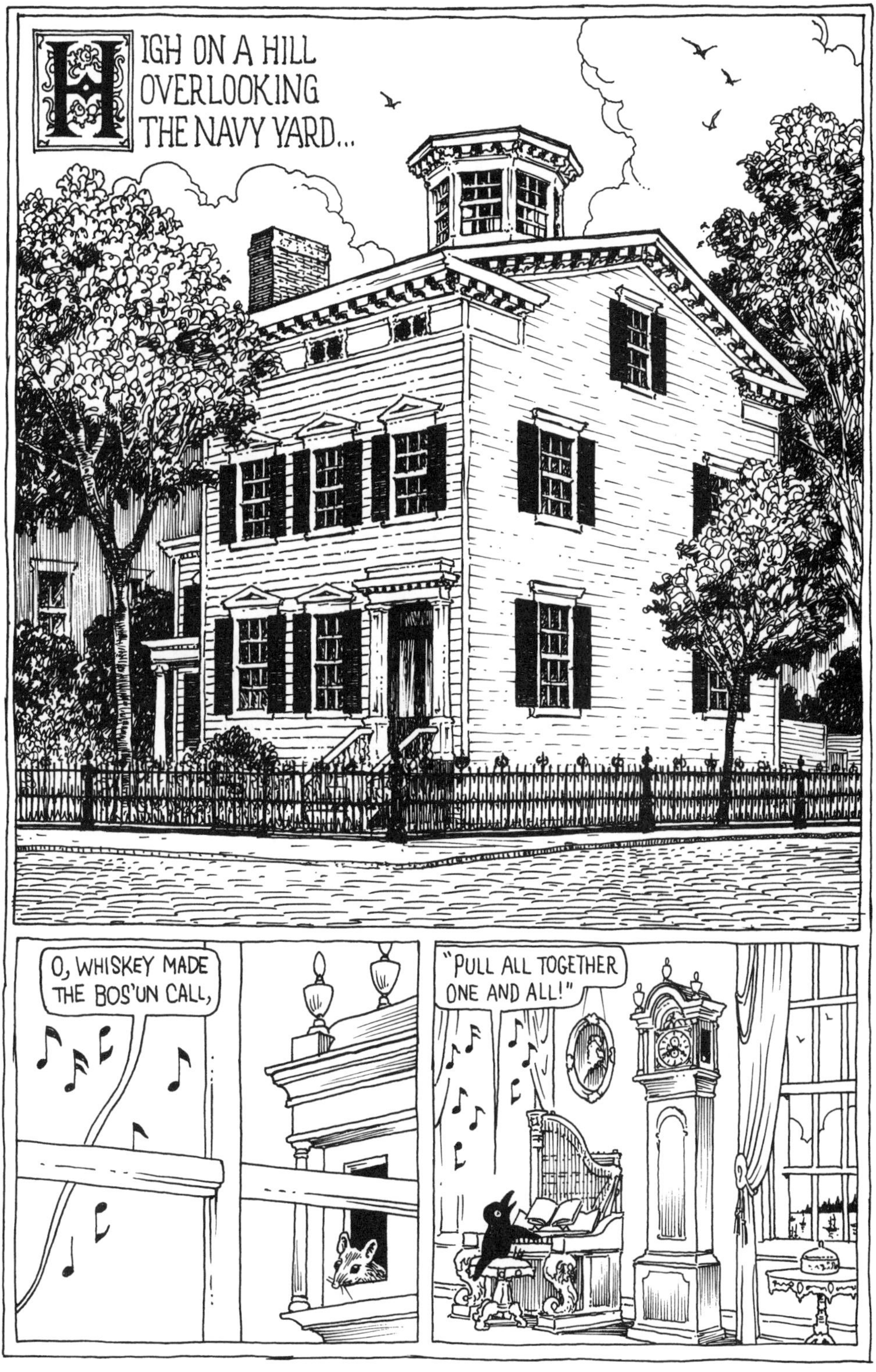
HIGH ON A HILL OVERLOOKING THE NAVY YARD...
O, WHISKEY MADE THE BOS'UN CALL,
"PULL ALL TOGETHER ONE AND ALL!"

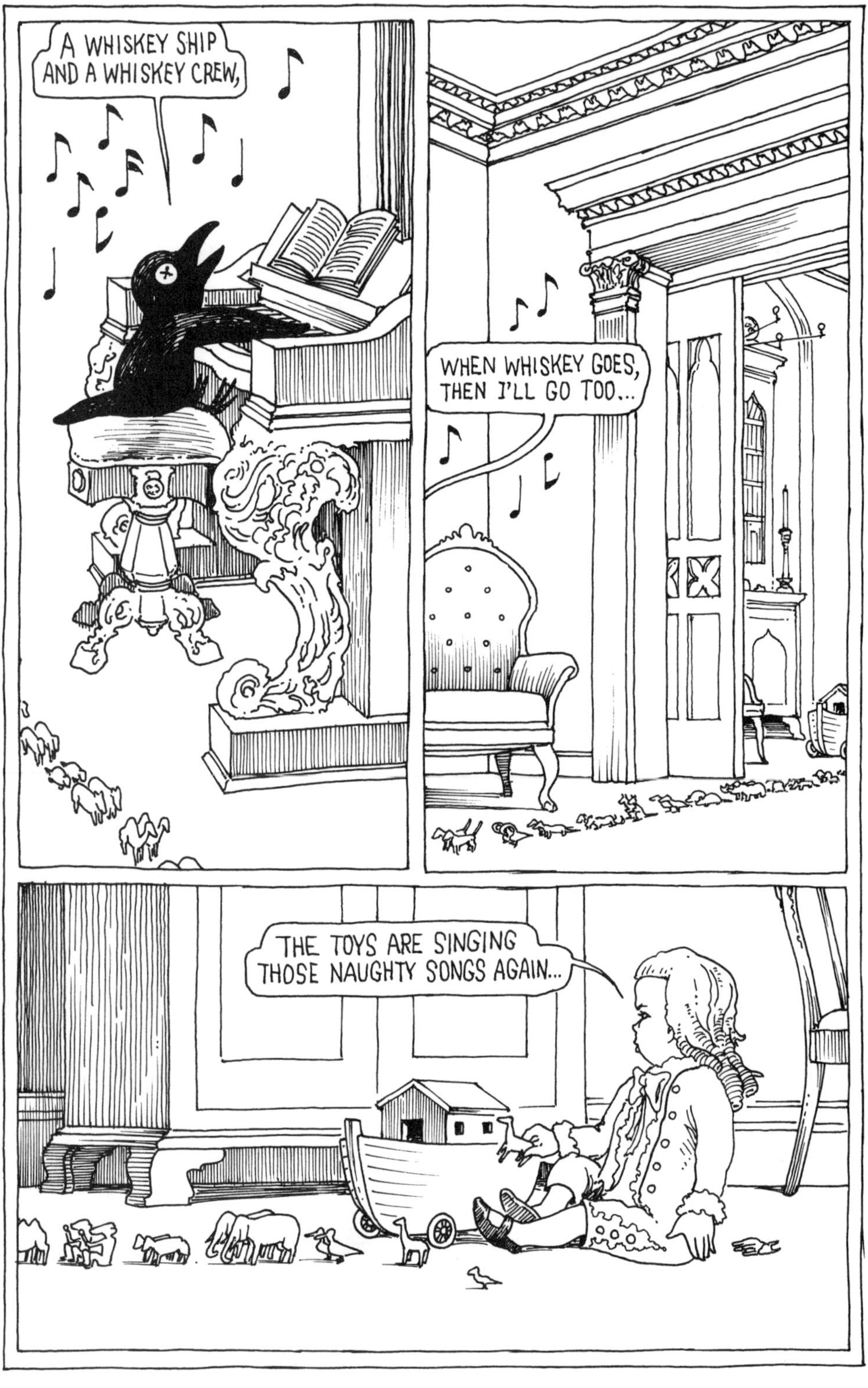
A WHISKEY SHIP AND A WHISKEY CREW,
WHEN WHISKEY GOES, THEN I'LL GO TOO...
THE TOYS ARE SINGING THOSE NAUGHTY SONGS AGAIN...

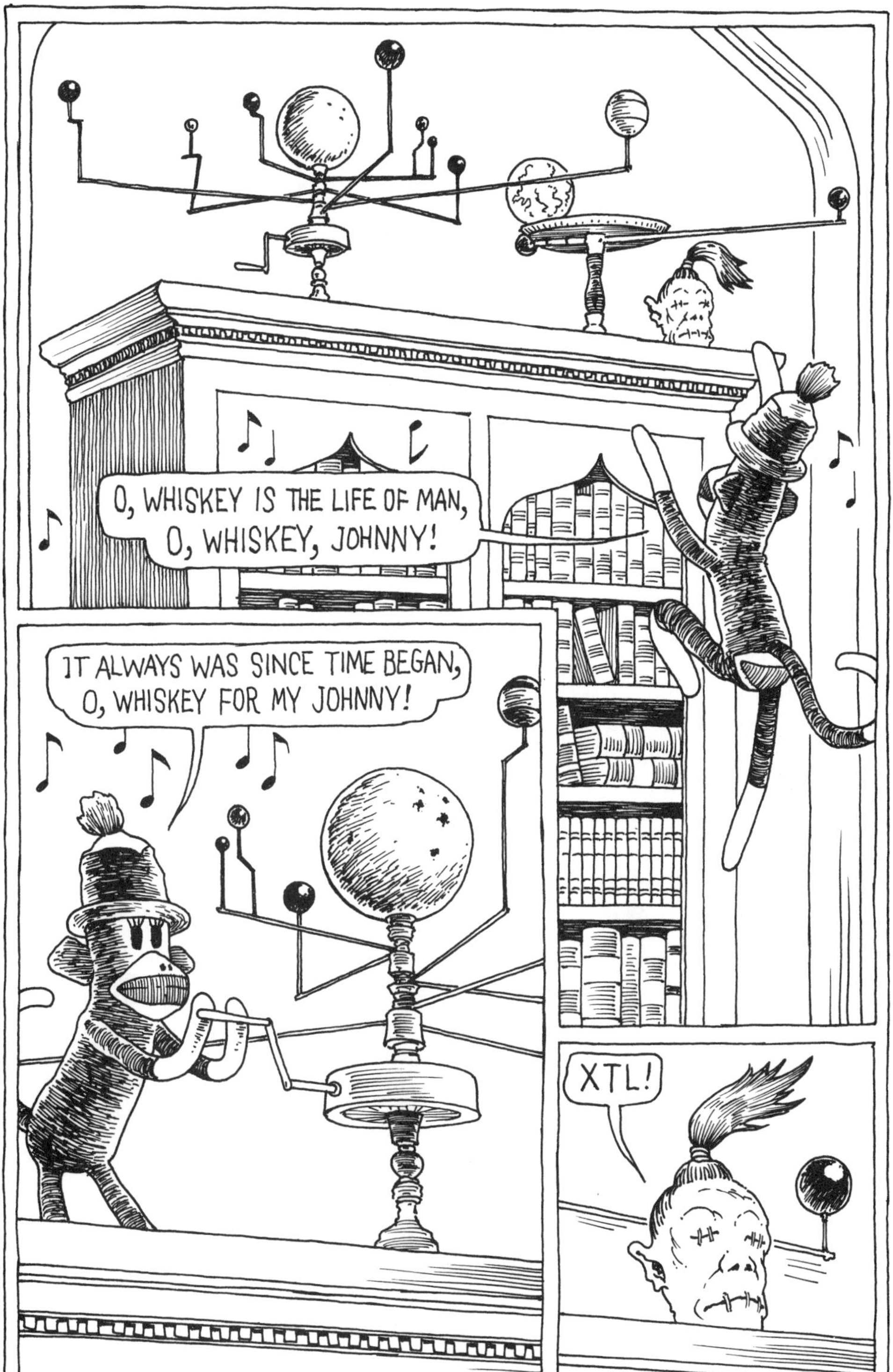
O, WHISKEY IS THE LIFE OF MAN,
O, WHISKEY, JOHNNY!
IT ALWAYS WAS SINCE TIME BEGAN,
O, WHISKEY FOR MY JOHNNY!
XTL!

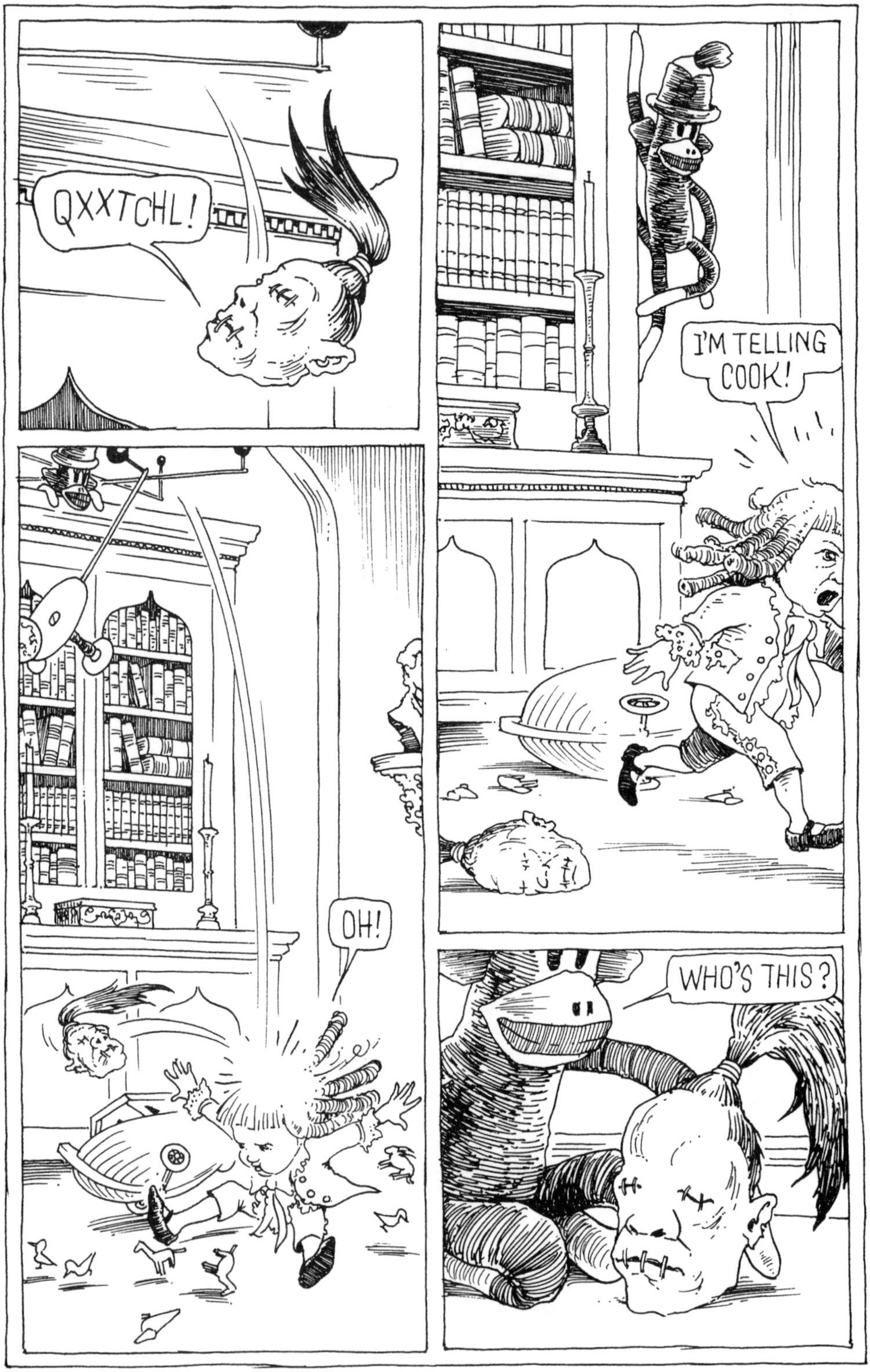
QXXTCHL!
I'M TELLING COOK!
OH!
WHO'S THIS?

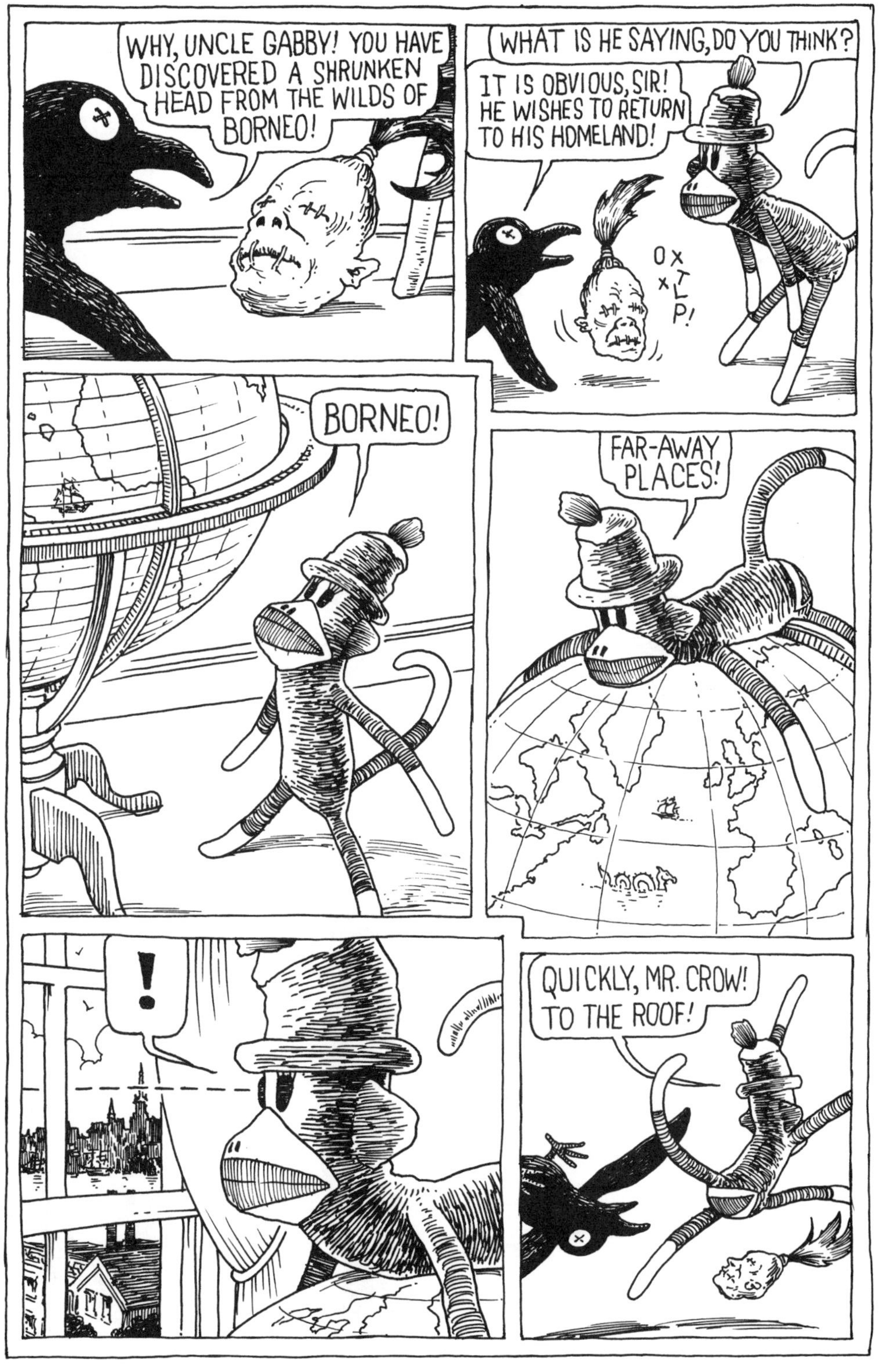

WHY, UNCLE GABBY! YOU HAVE DISCOVERED A SHRUNKEN HEAD FROM THE WILDS OF BORNEO!
WHAT IS HE SAYING, DO YOU THINK?
IT IS OBVIOUS, SIR! HE WISHES TO RETURN TO HIS HOMELAND!
OXTLP!
BORNEO!
FAR-AWAY PLACES!
!
QUICKLY, MR. CROW! TO THE ROOF!

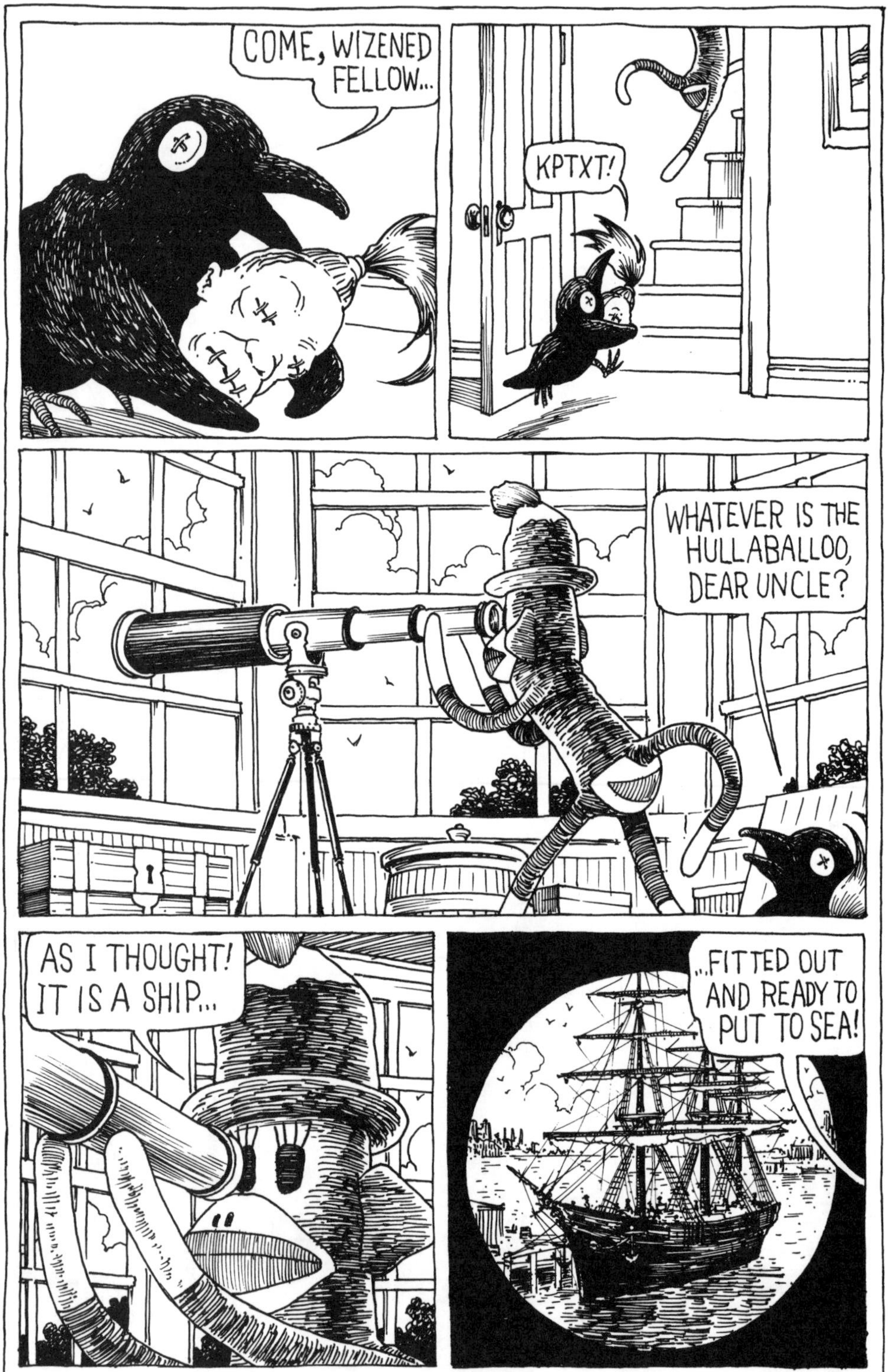
COME, WIZENED FELLOW...
KPTXT!
WHATEVER IS THE HULLABALLOO, DEAR UNCLE?
AS I THOUGHT! IT IS A SHIP...
...FITTED OUT AND READY TO PUT TO SEA!

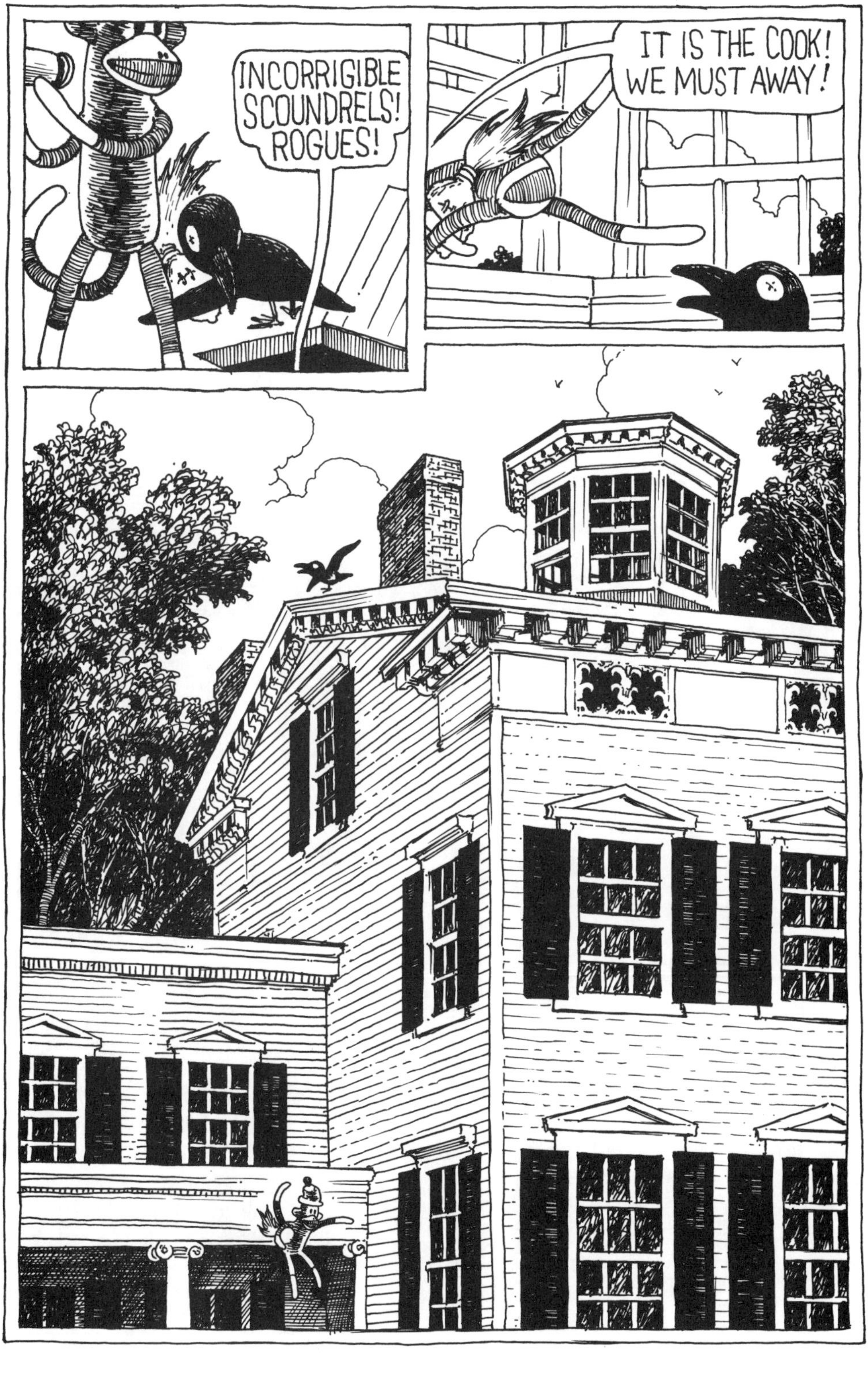
INCORRIGIBLE SCOUNDRELS! ROGUES!
IT IS THE COOK! WE MUST AWAY!

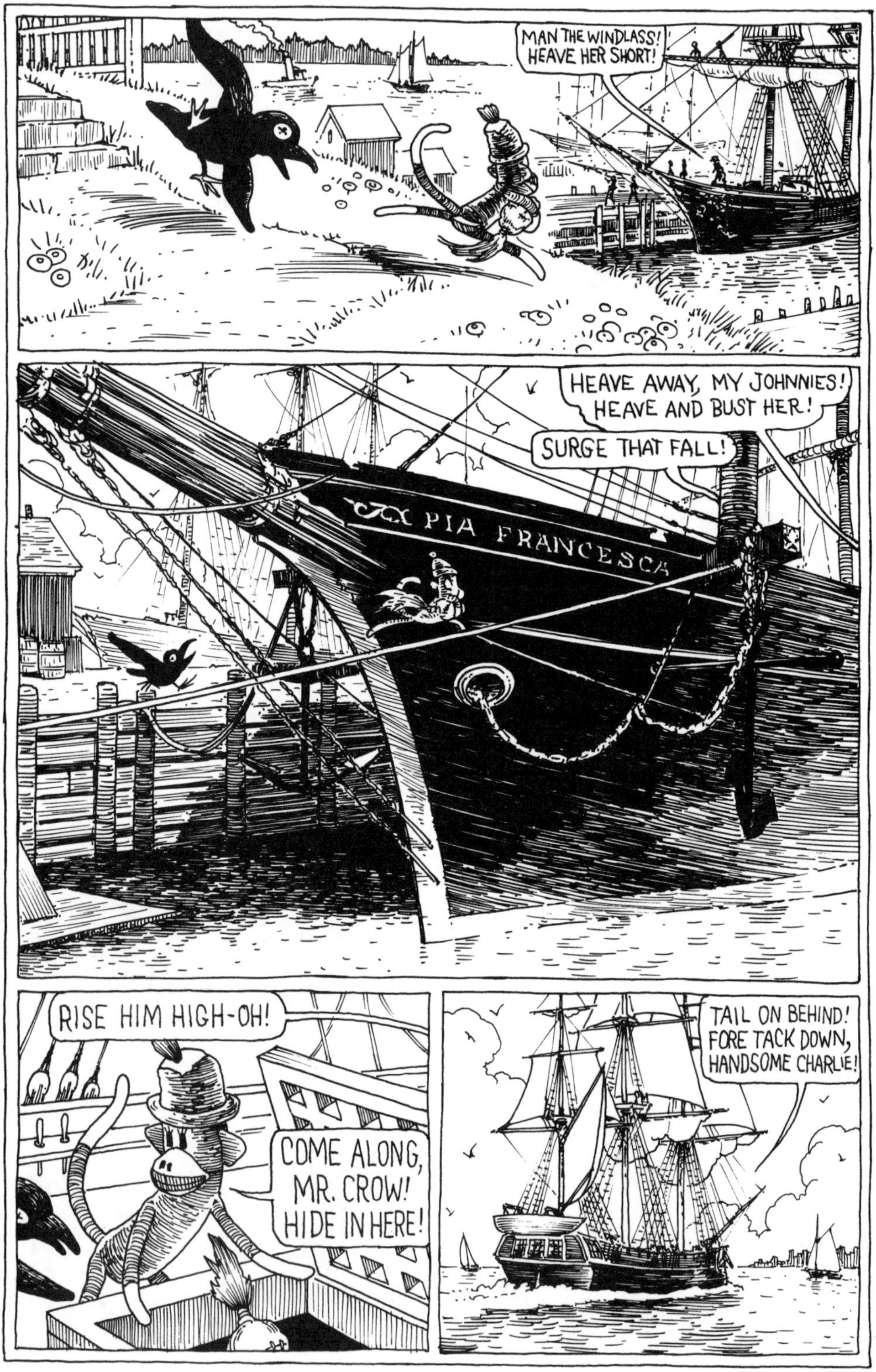
MAN THE WINDLASS! HEAVE HER SHORT!
HEAVE AWAY, MY JOHNNIES! HEAVE AND BUST HER!
SURGE THAT FALL!
PIA FRANCESCA
RISE HIM HIGH-OH!
COME ALONG, MR. CROW! HIDE IN HERE!
TAIL ON BEHIND! FORE TACK DOWN, HANDSOME CHARLIE!

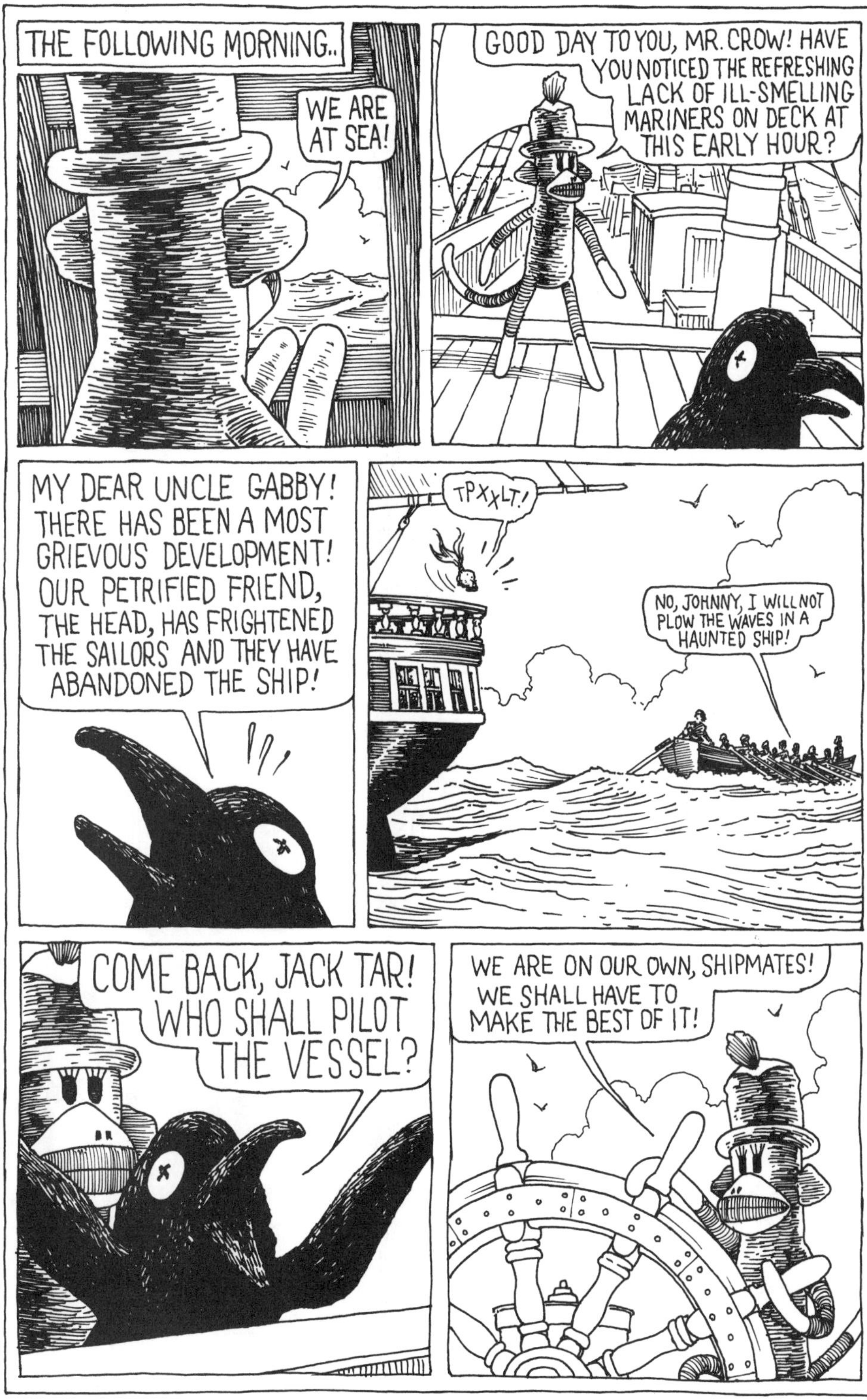
THE FOLLOWING MORNING..
WE ARE AT SEA!
GOOD DAY TO YOU, MR. CROW! HAVE YOU NOTICED THE REFRESHING LACK OF ILL-SMELLING MARINERS ON DECK AT THIS EARLY HOUR?
MY DEAR UNCLE GABBY! THERE HAS BEEN A MOST GRIEVOUS DEVELOPMENT! OUR PETRIFIED FRIEND, THE HEAD, HAS FRIGHTENED THE SAILORS AND THEY HAVE ABANDONED THE SHIP!
TPXXLT!
NO, JOHNNY, I WILL NOT PLOW THE WAVES IN A HAUNTED SHIP!
COME BACK, JACK TAR! WHO SHALL PILOT THE VESSEL?
WE ARE ON OUR OWN, SHIPMATES! WE SHALL HAVE TO MAKE THE BEST OF IT!

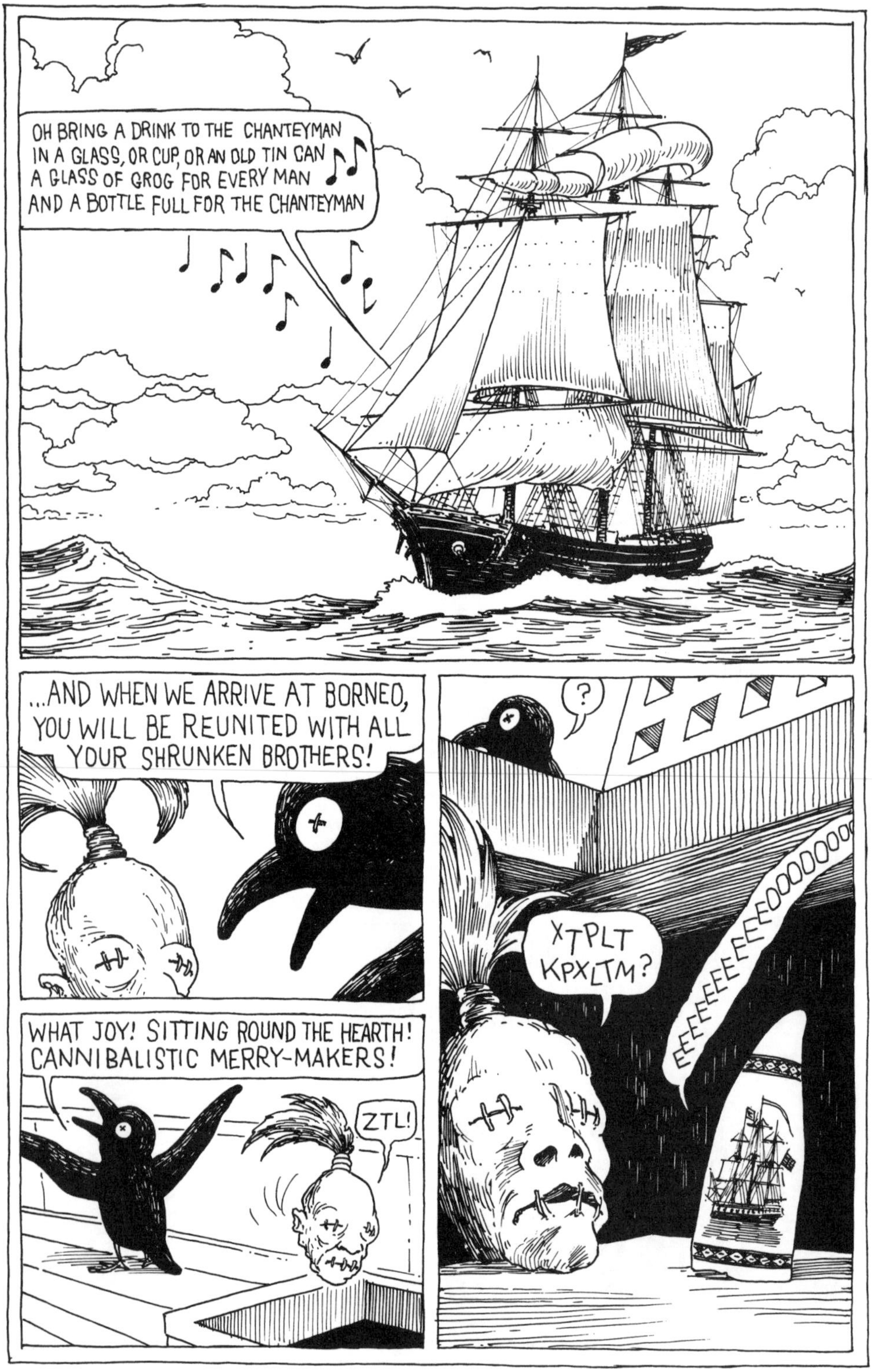
OH BRING A DRINK TO THE CHANTEYMAN
IN A GLASS, OR CUP, OR AN OLD TIN CAN
A GLASS OF GROG FOR EVERY MAN
AND A BOTTLE FULL FOR THE CHANTEYMAN
...AND WHEN WE ARRIVE AT BORNEO, YOU WILL BE REUNITED WITH ALL YOUR SHRUNKEN BROTHERS!
WHAT JOY! SITTING ROUND THE HEARTH! CANNIBALISTIC MERRY-MAKERS!
ZTL!
?
XTPLT KPXLTM?
EEEEEEEEEEOOOOOOOOO

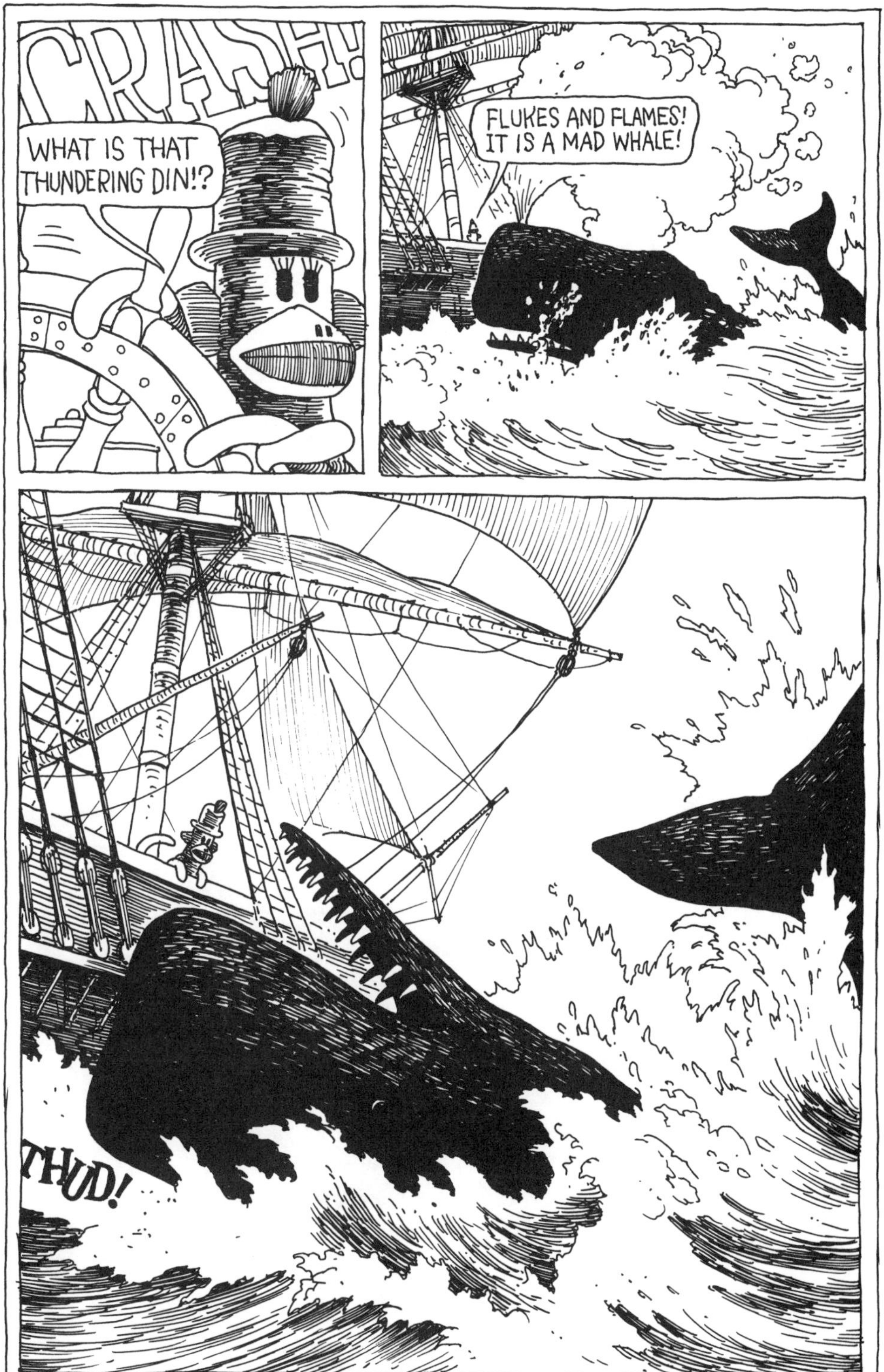
CRASH!
WHAT IS THAT THUNDERING DIN!?
FLUKES AND FLAMES! IT IS A MAD WHALE!
THUD!

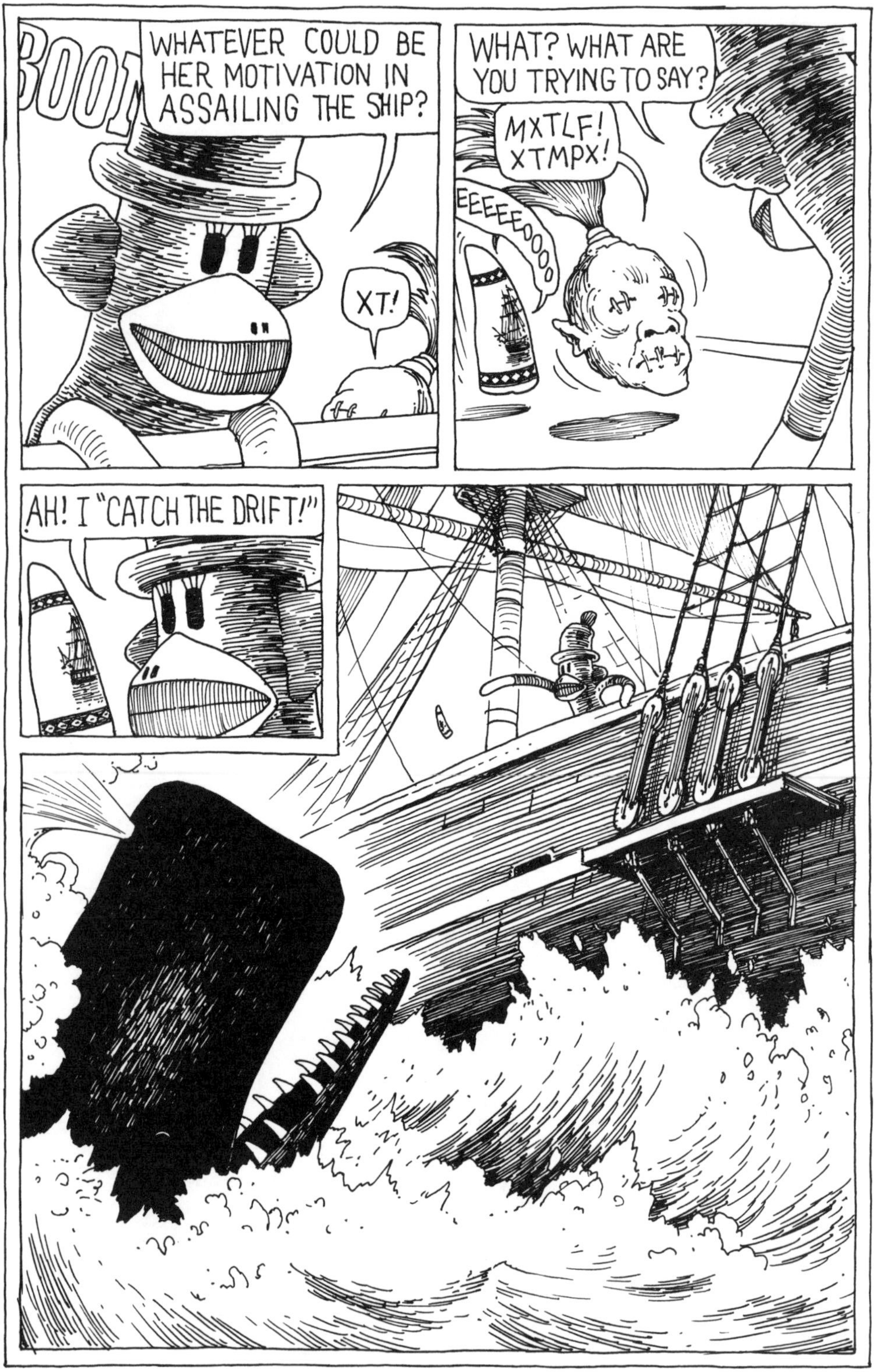
BOOM
WHATEVER COULD BE HER MOTIVATION IN ASSAILING THE SHIP?
XT!
WHAT? WHAT ARE YOU TRYING TO SAY?
MXTLF! XTMPX!
EEEEEEOOOOO
AH! I "CATCH THE DRIFT!"

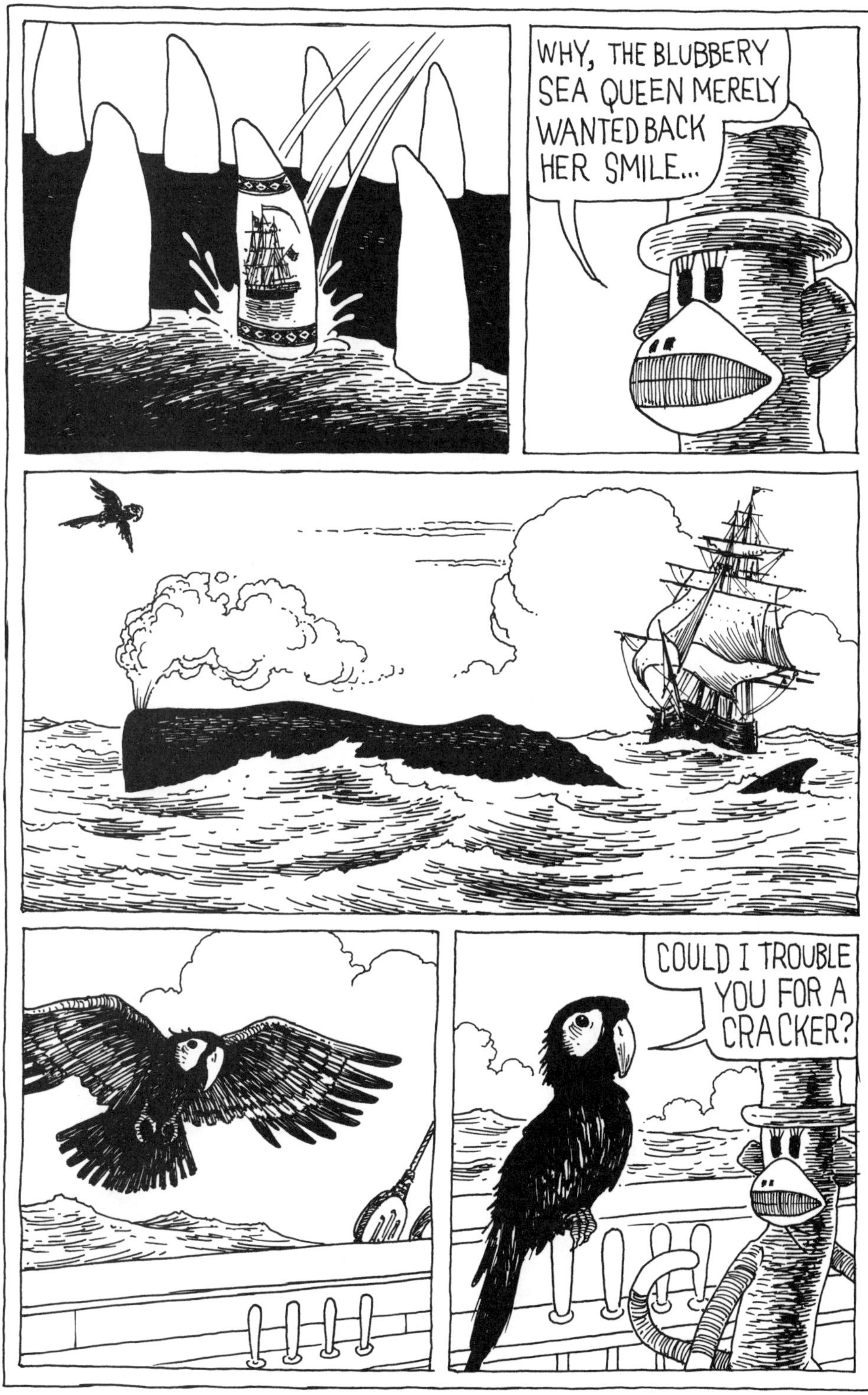
WHY, THE BLUBBERY SEA QUEEN MERELY WANTED BACK HER SMILE...
COULD I TROUBLE YOU FOR A CRACKER?

IF YOU CAN FIND A CRACKER ABOARD THE SHIP, SIR, YOU MAY CERTAINLY HAVE ONE

THAT IS MOST WELCOME NEWS, AS I WANT A CRACKER!

YOU SEEM TO BE NATIVE TO THIS REGION, SIR! COULD YOU HELP US TO FIX OUR POSITION? WE SEEK THE BORNEO

WHY, THAT IS BORNEO, MY DEAR FELLOW, A MILE TO LEEWARD!

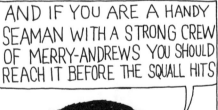

AND IF YOU ARE A HANDY SEAMAN WITH A STRONG CREW OF MERRY-ANDREWS YOU SHOULD REACH IT BEFORE THE SQUALL HITS

WHAT IS A "SQUALL"?

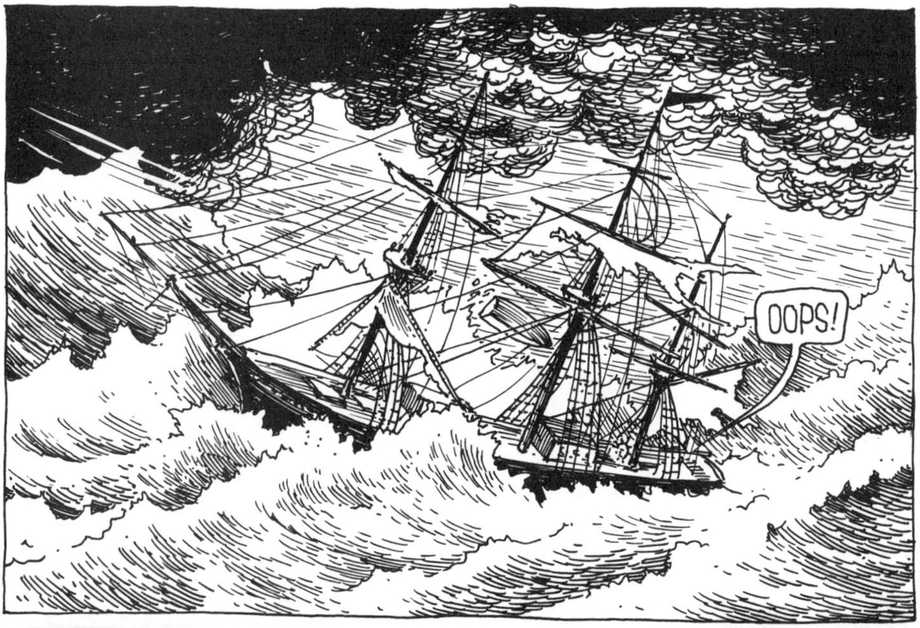
OOPS!

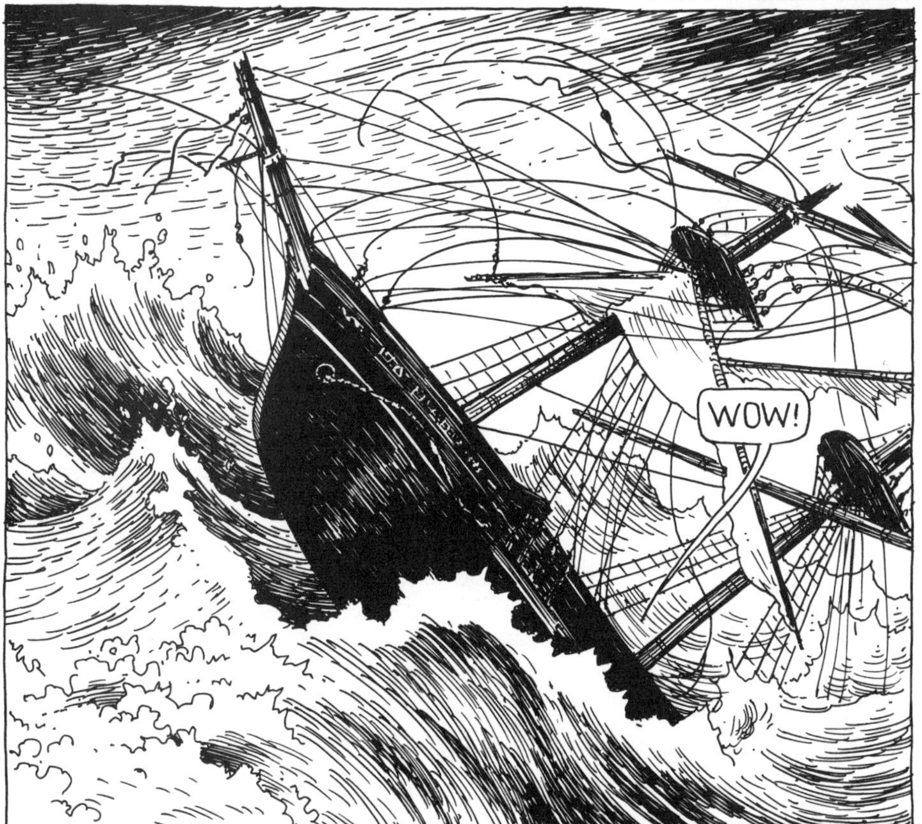
WOW!

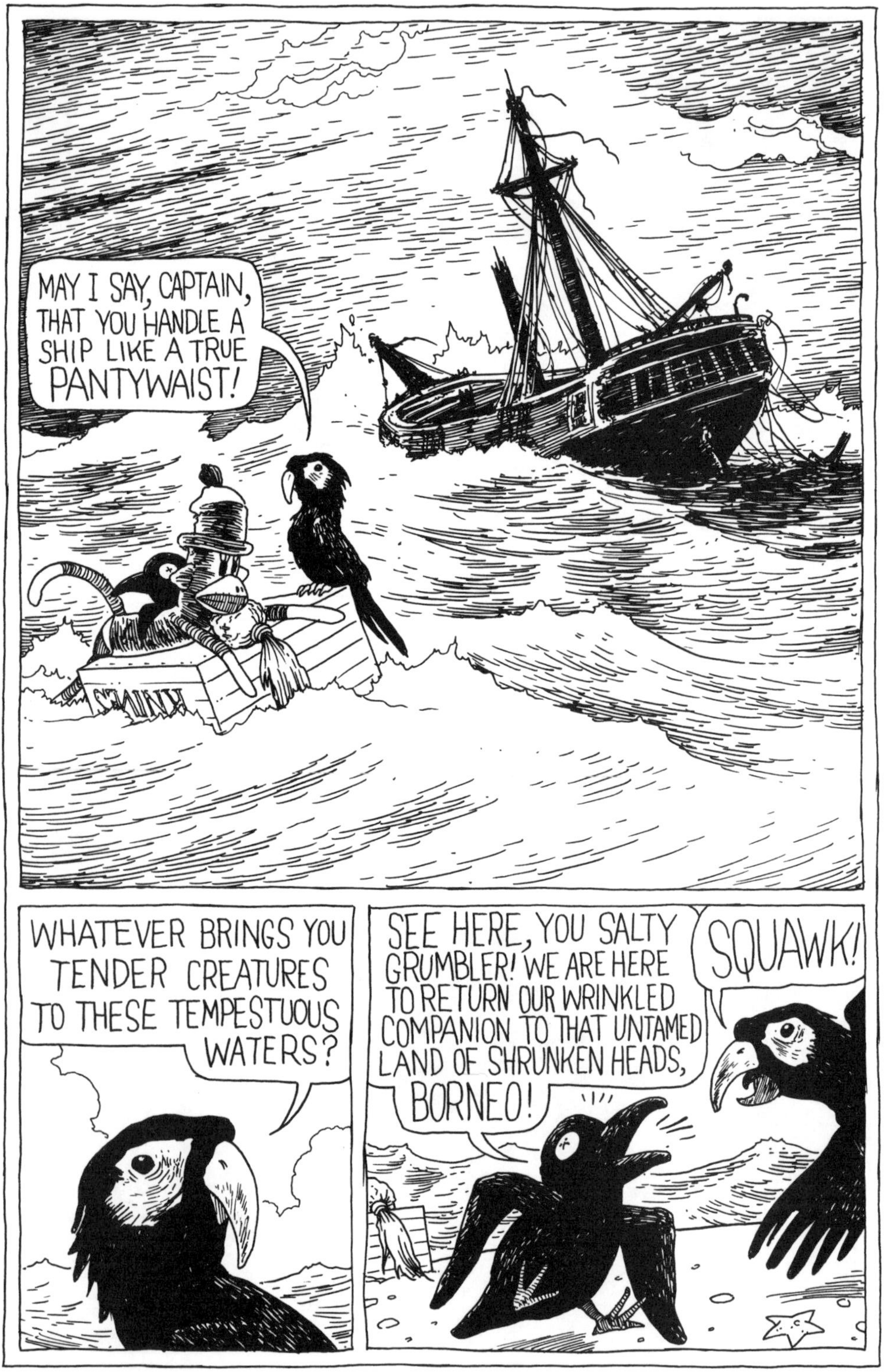
MAY I SAY, CAPTAIN, THAT YOU HANDLE A SHIP LIKE A TRUE PANTYWAIST!
WHATEVER BRINGS YOU TENDER CREATURES TO THESE TEMPESTUOUS WATERS?
SEE HERE, YOU SALTY GRUMBLER! WE ARE HERE TO RETURN OUR WRINKLED COMPANION TO THAT UNTAMED LAND OF SHRUNKEN HEADS, BORNEO!
SQUAWK!

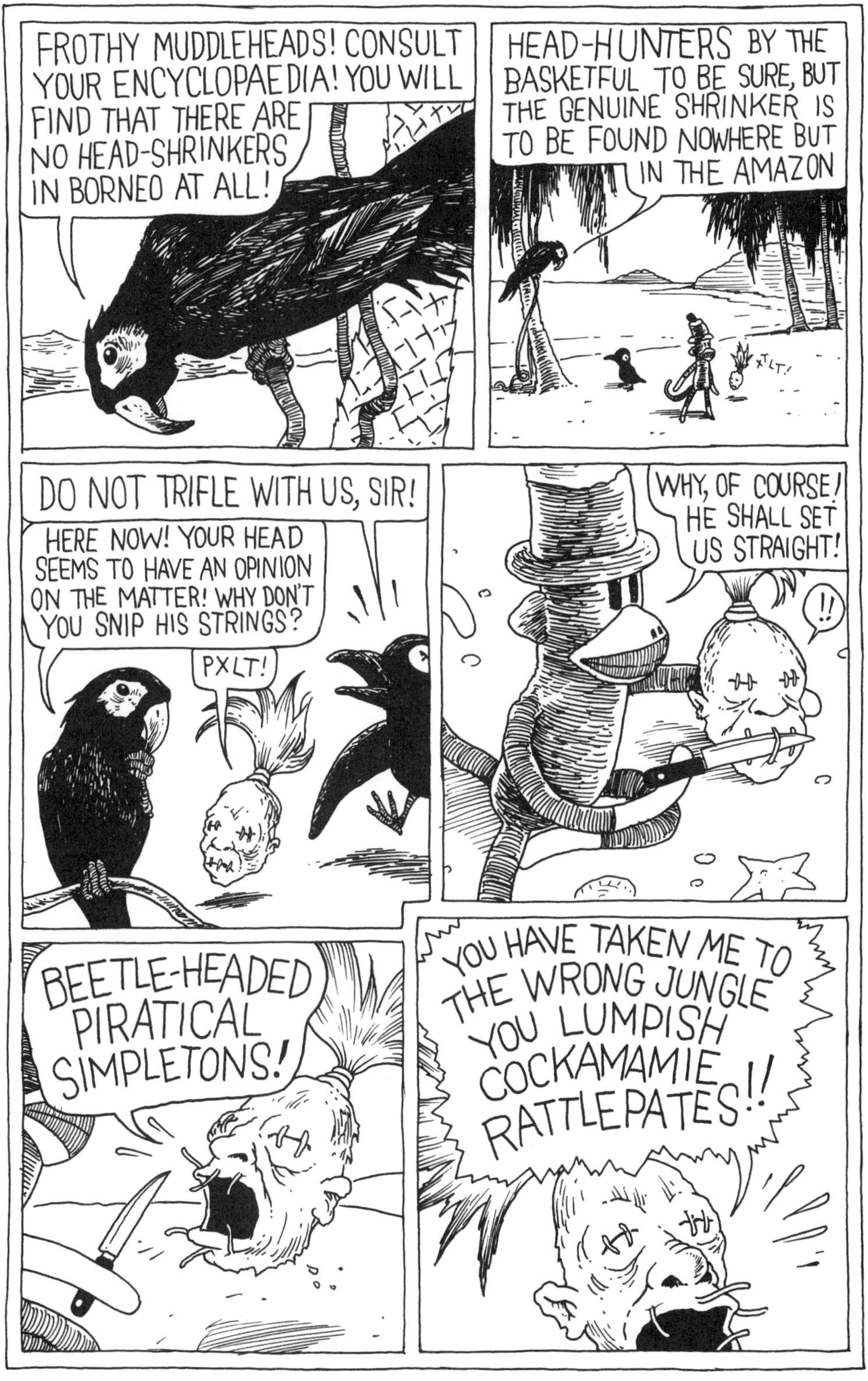
FROTHY MUDDLEHEADS! CONSULT YOUR ENCYCLOPAEDIA! YOU WILL FIND THAT THERE ARE NO HEAD-SHRINKERS IN BORNEO AT ALL!
HEAD-HUNTERS BY THE BASKETFUL TO BE SURE, BUT THE GENUINE SHRINKER IS TO BE FOUND NOWHERE BUT IN THE AMAZON
XTLT!
DO NOT TRIFLE WITH US, SIR!
HERE NOW! YOUR HEAD SEEMS TO HAVE AN OPINION ON THE MATTER! WHY DON'T YOU SNIP HIS STRINGS?
PXLT!
WHY, OF COURSE! HE SHALL SET US STRAIGHT!
!!
BEETLE-HEADED PIRATICAL SIMPLETONS!
YOU HAVE TAKEN ME TO THE WRONG JUNGLE YOU LUMPISH COCKAMAMIE RATTLEPATES!!

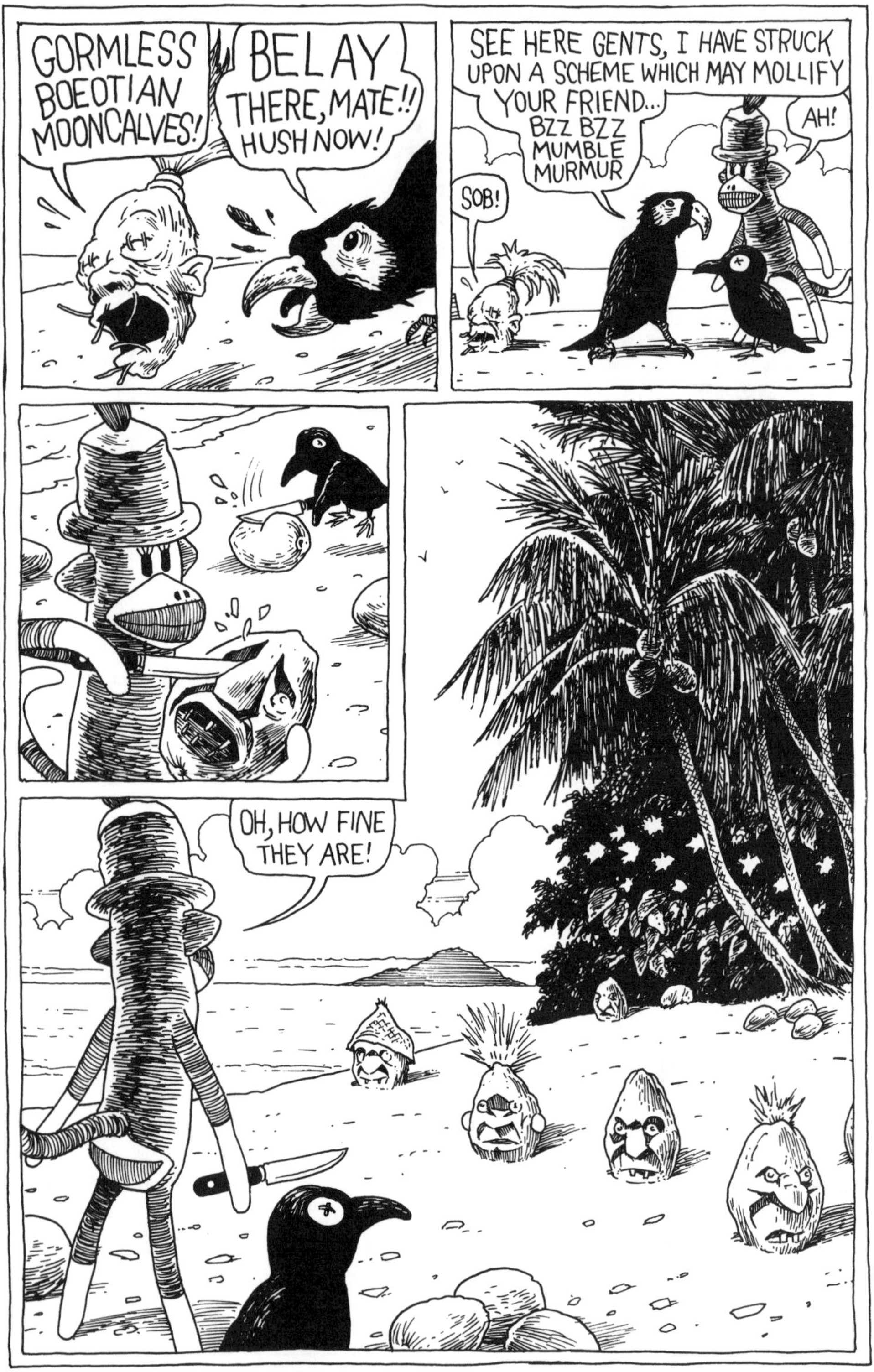
GORMLESS BOEOTIAN MOONCALVES!
BELAY THERE, MATE!! HUSH NOW!
SEE HERE GENTS, I HAVE STRUCK UPON A SCHEME WHICH MAY MOLLIFY YOUR FRIEND...
BZZ BZZ MUMBLE MURMUR
AH!
SOB!
OH, HOW FINE THEY ARE!

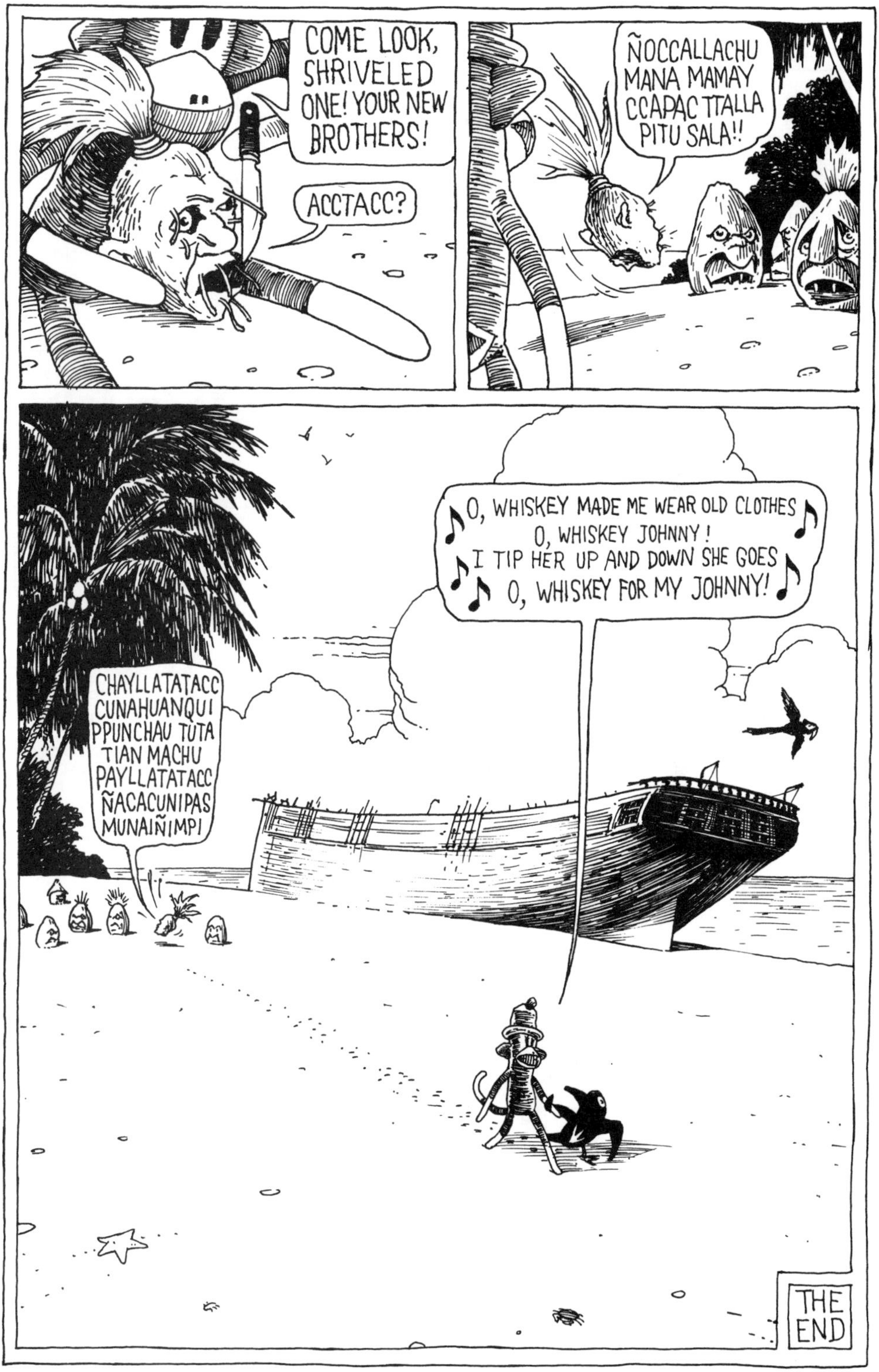
COME LOOK, SHRIVELED ONE! YOUR NEW BROTHERS!
ACCTACC?
ÑOCCALLACHU MANA MAMAY CCAPAC TTALLA PITU SALA!!
O, WHISKEY MADE ME WEAR OLD CLOTHES
O, WHISKEY JOHNNY!
I TIP HER UP AND DOWN SHE GOES
O, WHISKEY FOR MY JOHNNY!
CHAYLLATATACC CUNAHUANQUI PPUNCHAU TUTA TIAN MACHU PAYLLATATACC ÑACACUNIPAS MUNAIÑIMPI
THE END

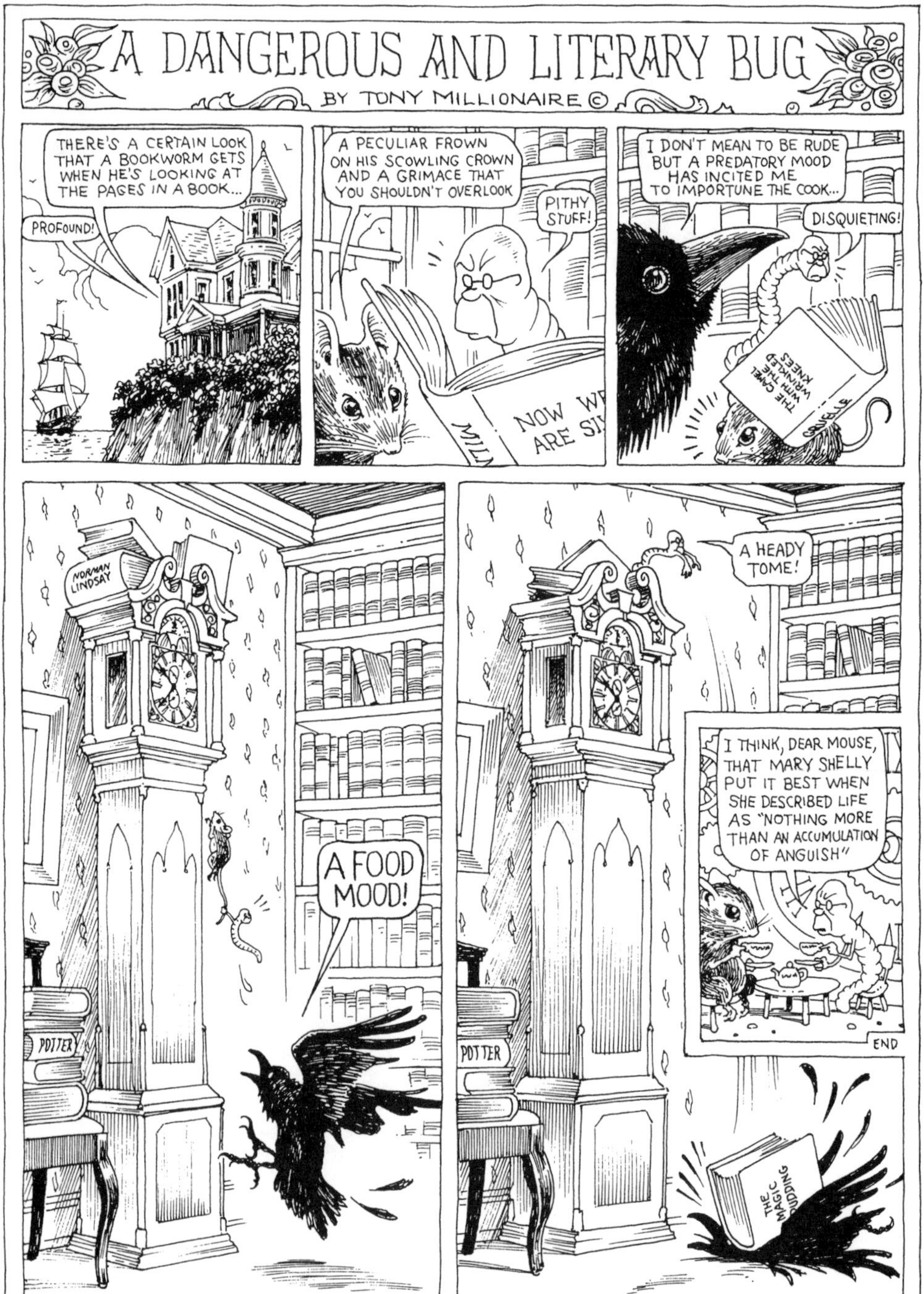
A DANGEROUS AND LITERARY BUG
BY TONY MILLIONAIRE ©
THERE'S A CERTAIN LOOK THAT A BOOKWORM GETS WHEN HE'S LOOKING AT THE PAGES IN A BOOK...
PROFOUND!
A PECULIAR FROWN ON HIS SCOWLING CROWN AND A GRIMACE THAT YOU SHOULDN'T OVERLOOK
PITHY STUFF!
NOW WE ARE SI
I DON'T MEAN TO BE RUDE BUT A PREDATORY MOOD HAS INCITED ME TO IMPORTUNE THE COOK...
DISQUIETING!
THE CAMEL WITH THE WRINKLED KNEES
GRUELLE
NORMAN LINDSAY
POTTER
A FOOD MOOD!
A HEADY TOME!
I THINK, DEAR MOUSE, THAT MARY SHELLY PUT IT BEST WHEN SHE DESCRIBED LIFE AS "NOTHING MORE THAN AN ACCUMULATION OF ANGUISH"
END
POTTER
THE MAGIC PUDDING

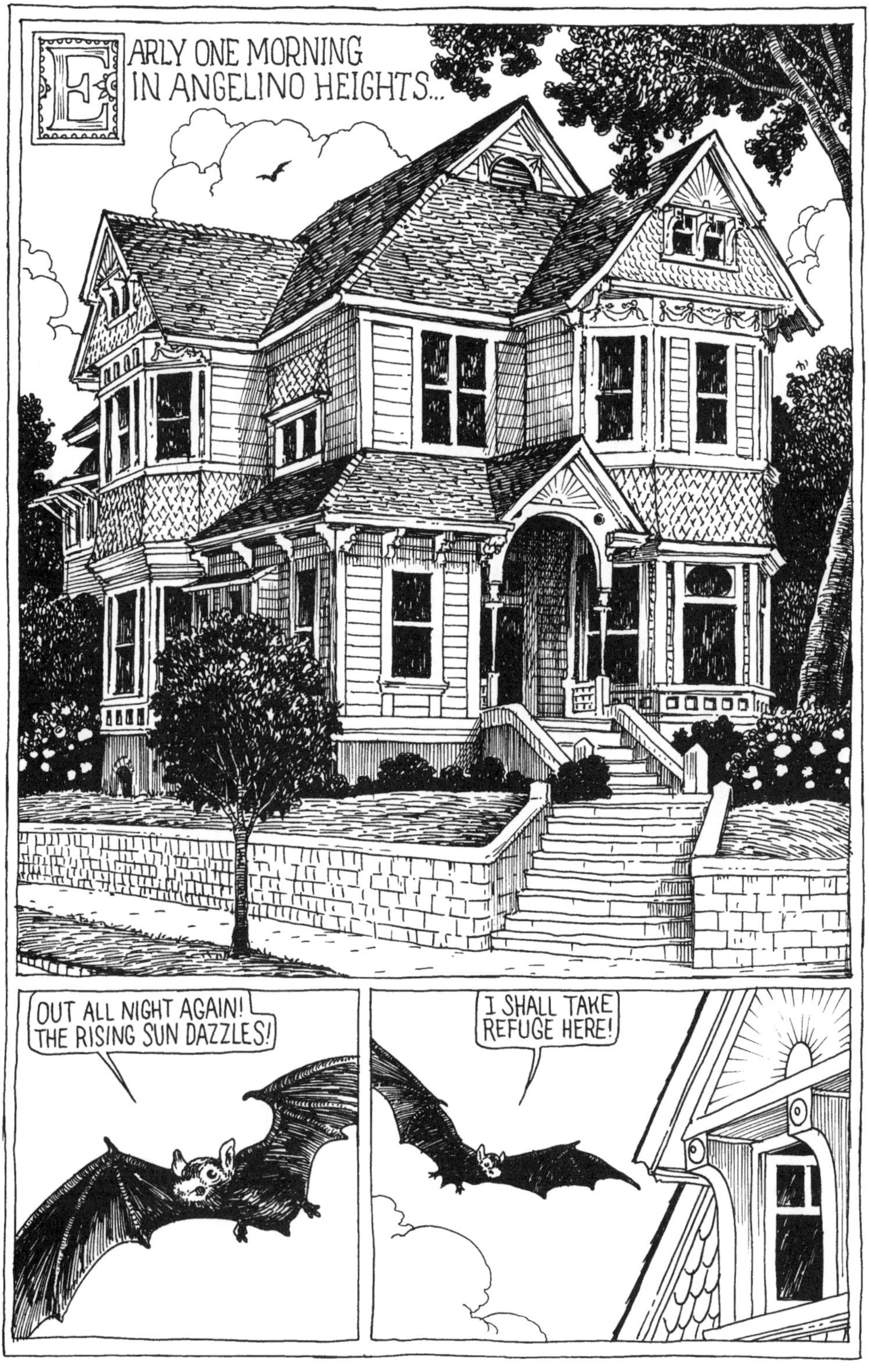
EARLY ONE MORNING IN ANGELINO HEIGHTS...
OUT ALL NIGHT AGAIN! THE RISING SUN DAZZLES!
I SHALL TAKE REFUGE HERE!

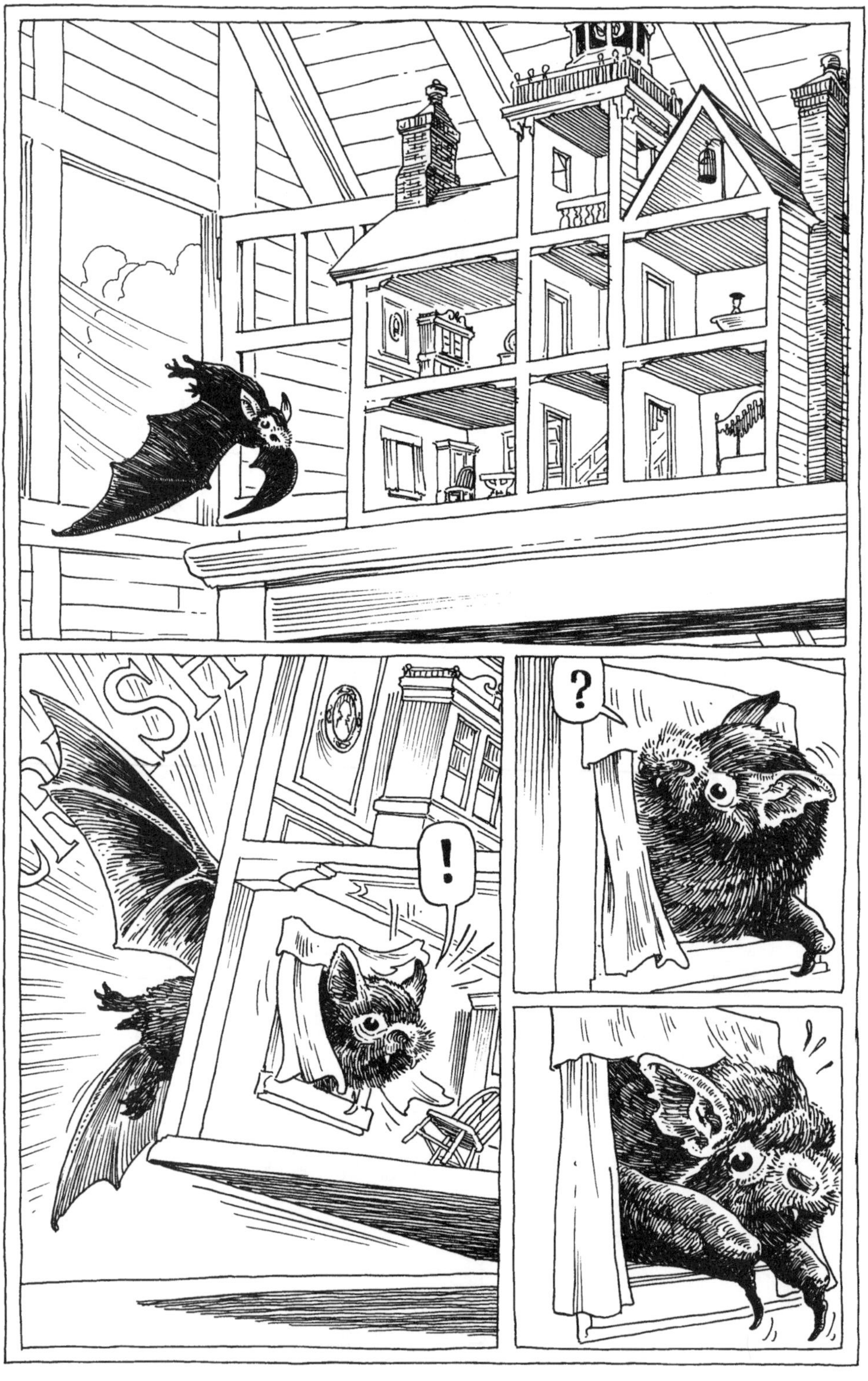
!
?

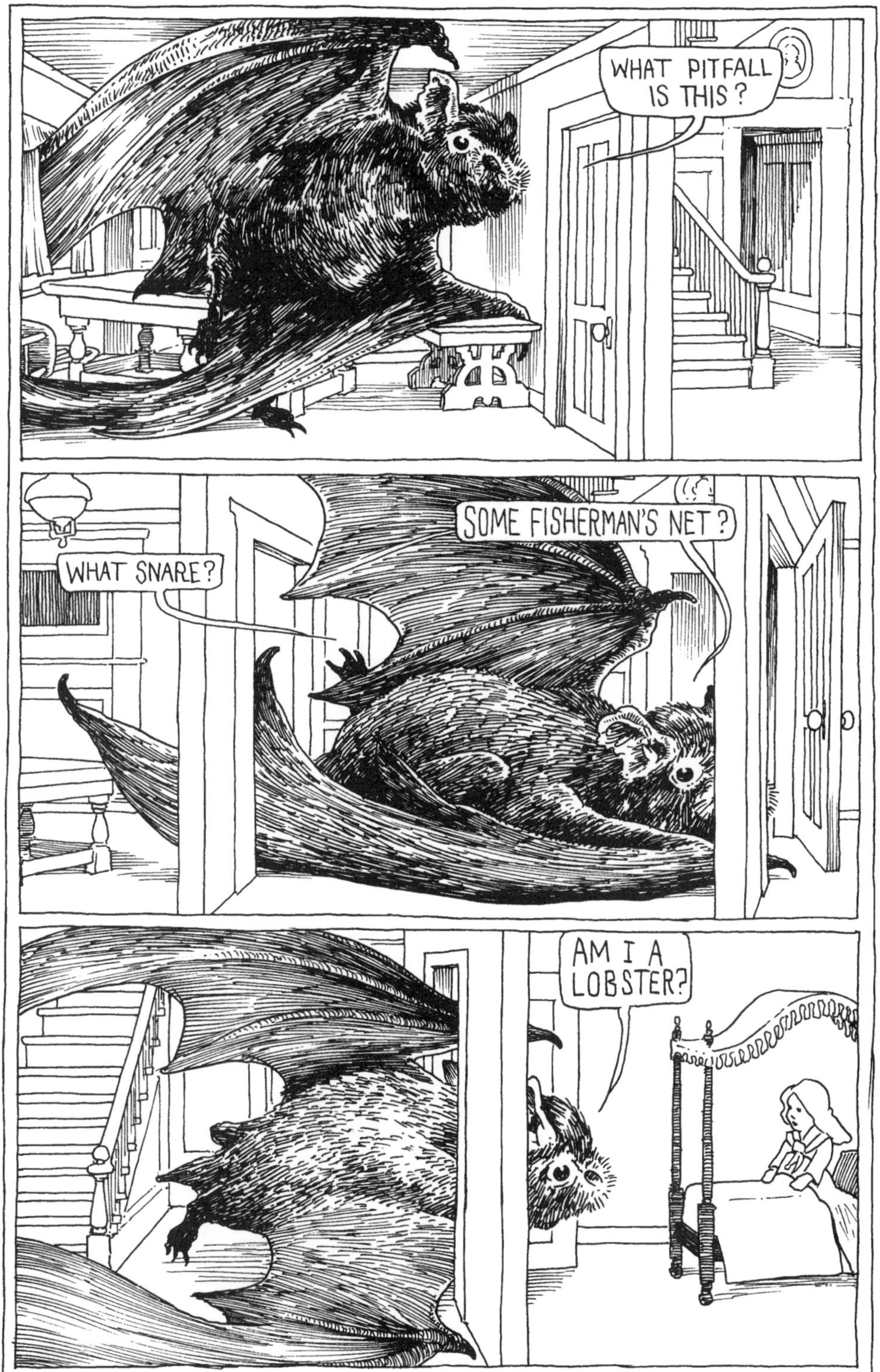
WHAT PITFALL IS THIS?
WHAT SNARE?
SOME FISHERMAN'S NET?
AM I A LOBSTER?

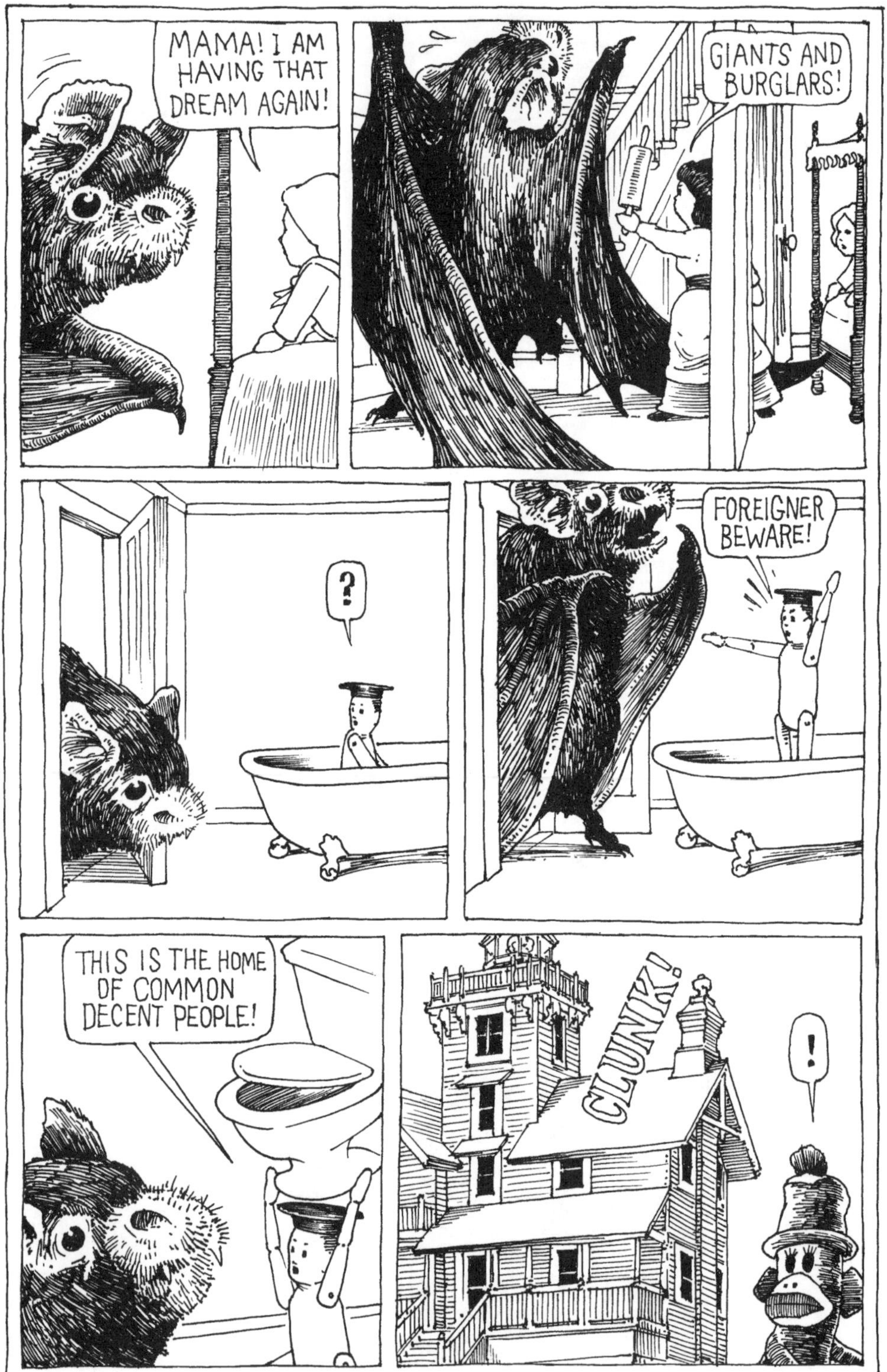
MAMA! I AM HAVING THAT DREAM AGAIN!
GIANTS AND BURGLARS!
?
FOREIGNER BEWARE!
THIS IS THE HOME OF COMMON DECENT PEOPLE!
CLUNK!
!

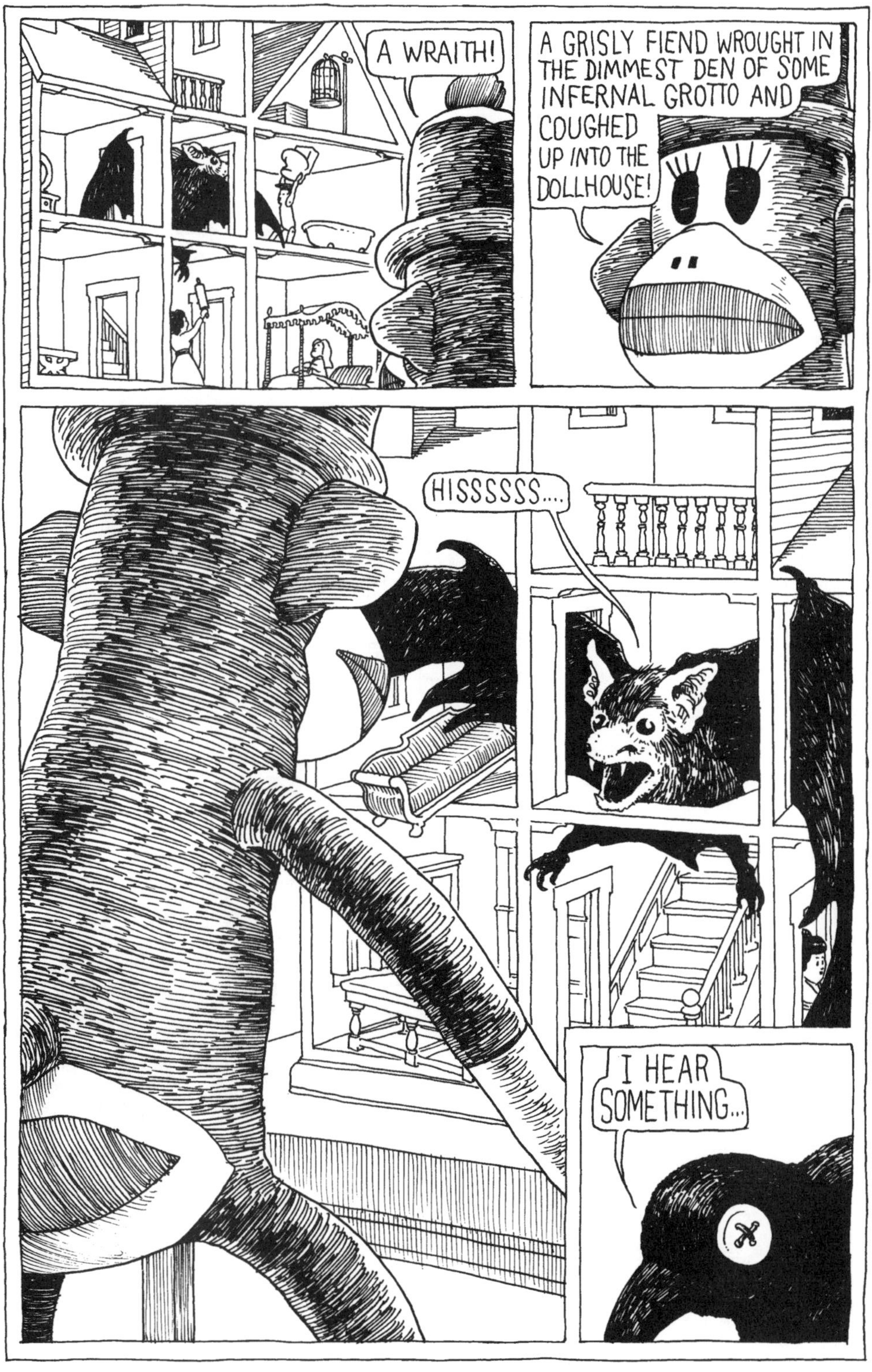
A WRAITH!
A GRISLY FIEND WROUGHT IN THE DIMMEST DEN OF SOME INFERNAL GROTTO AND COUGHED UP INTO THE DOLLHOUSE!
HISSSSSS....
I HEAR SOMETHING...

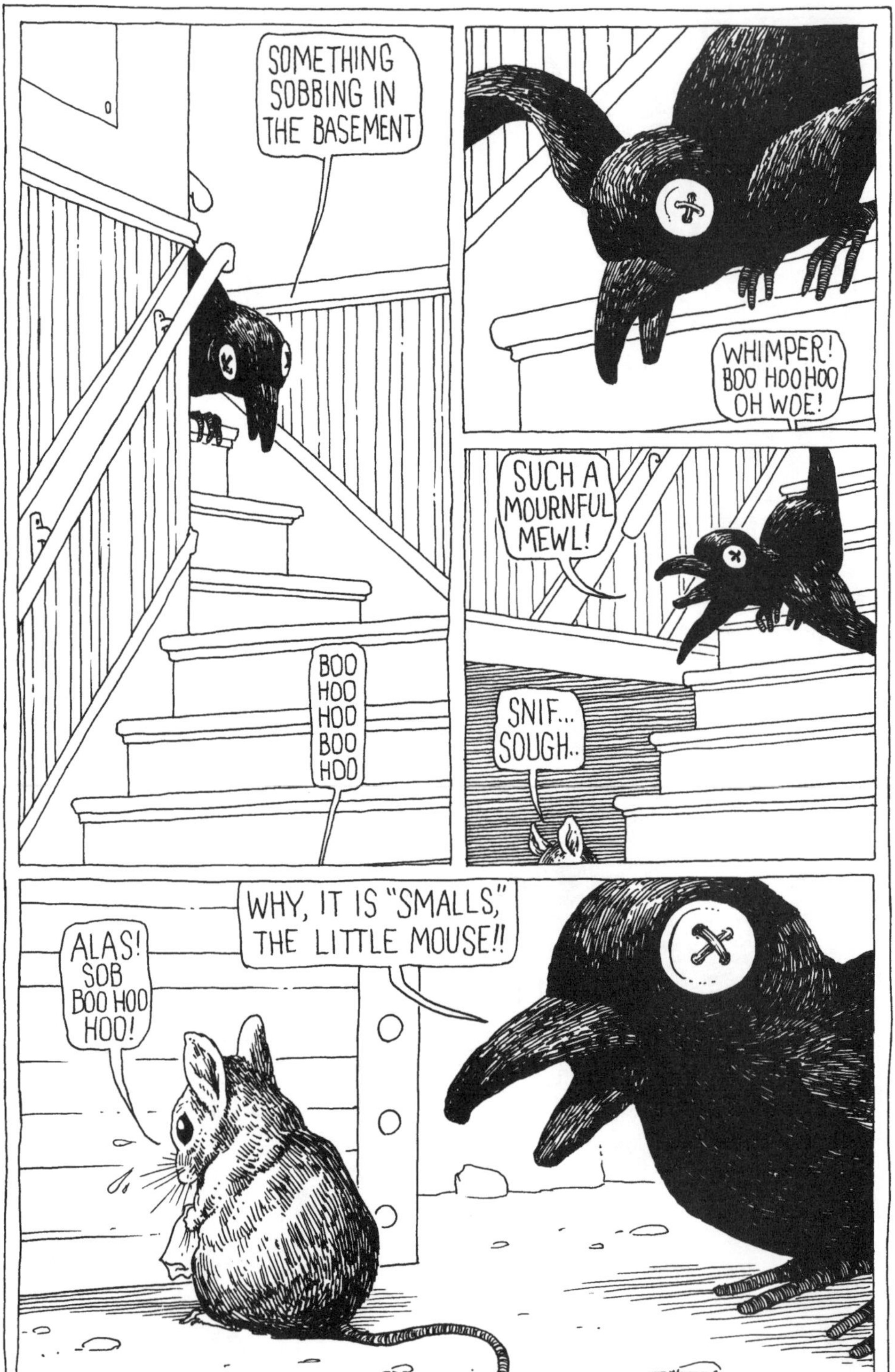
SOMETHING SOBBING IN THE BASEMENT
BOO HOO HOO BOO HOO
WHIMPER! BOO HOO HOO OH WOE!
SUCH A MOURNFUL MEWL!
SNIF... SOUGH..
ALAS! SOB BOO HOO HOO!
WHY, IT IS "SMALLS," THE LITTLE MOUSE!!

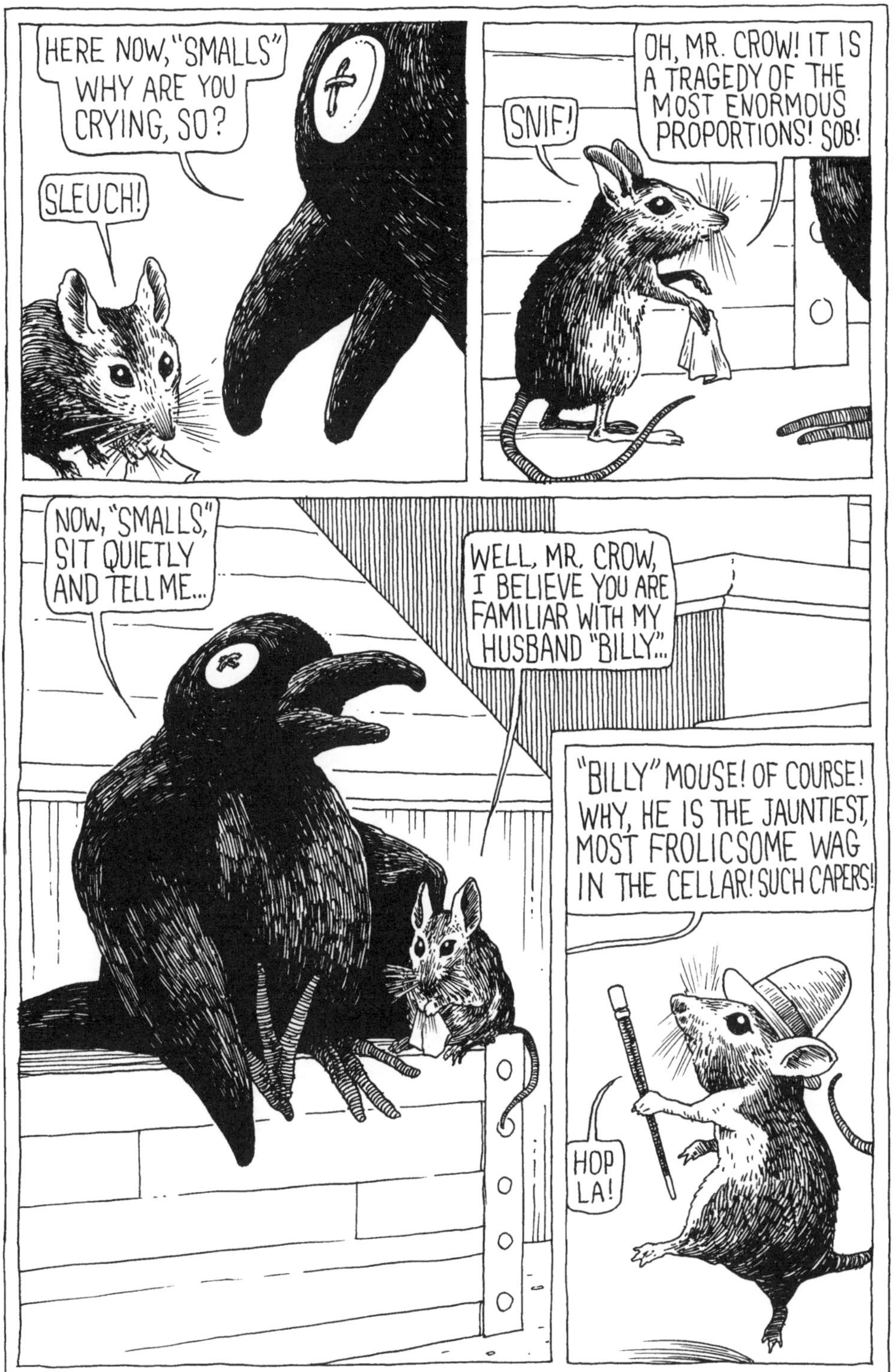
HERE NOW, "SMALLS" WHY ARE YOU CRYING, SO?
SLEUCH!
SNIF!
OH, MR. CROW! IT IS A TRAGEDY OF THE MOST ENORMOUS PROPORTIONS! SOB!
NOW, "SMALLS," SIT QUIETLY AND TELL ME...
WELL, MR. CROW, I BELIEVE YOU ARE FAMILIAR WITH MY HUSBAND "BILLY."...
"BILLY" MOUSE! OF COURSE! WHY, HE IS THE JAUNTIEST, MOST FROLICSOME WAG IN THE CELLAR! SUCH CAPERS!
HOP LA!

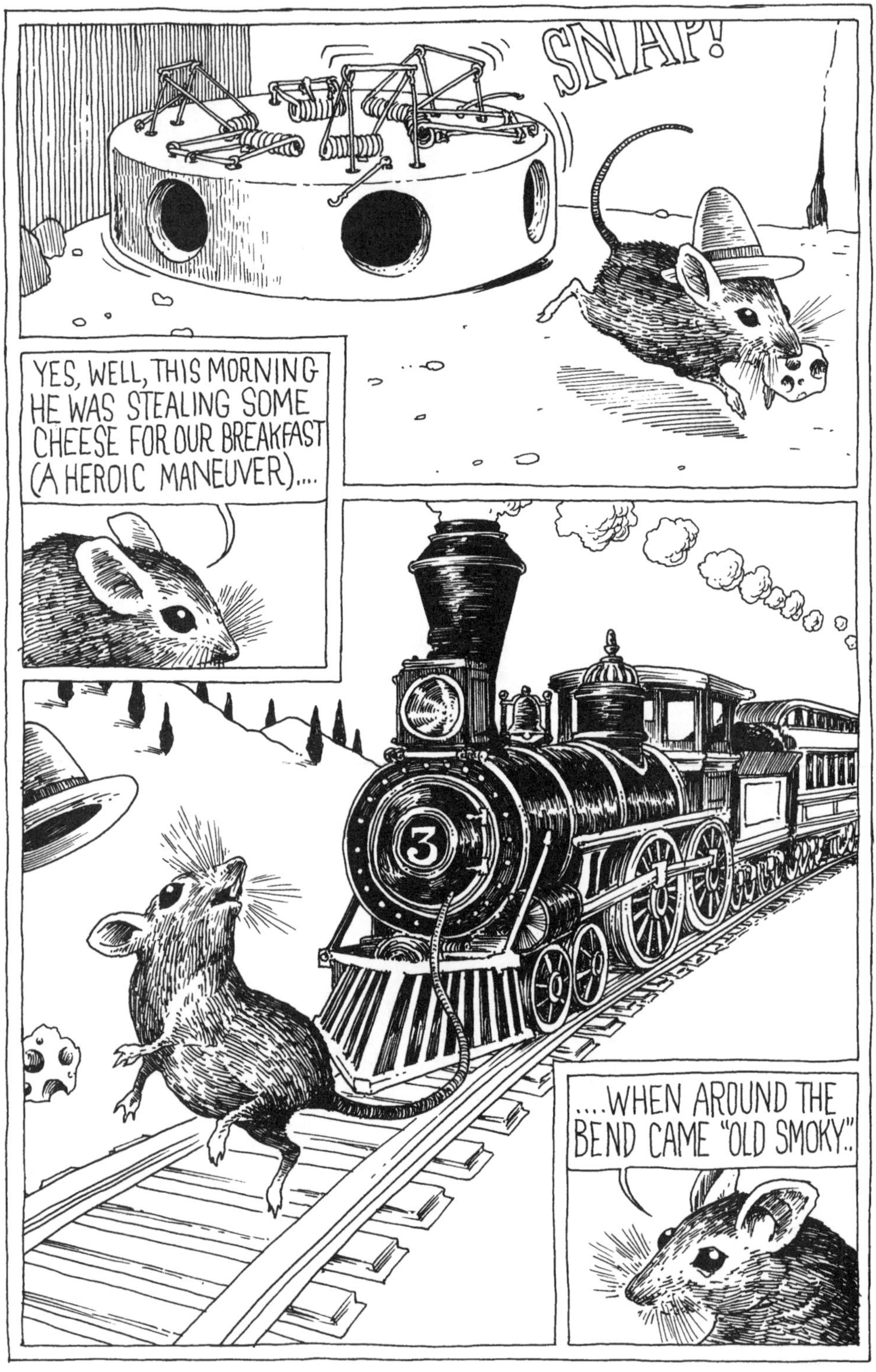
SNAP!
YES, WELL, THIS MORNING HE WAS STEALING SOME CHEESE FOR OUR BREAKFAST (A HEROIC MANEUVER)....
3
....WHEN AROUND THE BEND CAME "OLD SMOKY."

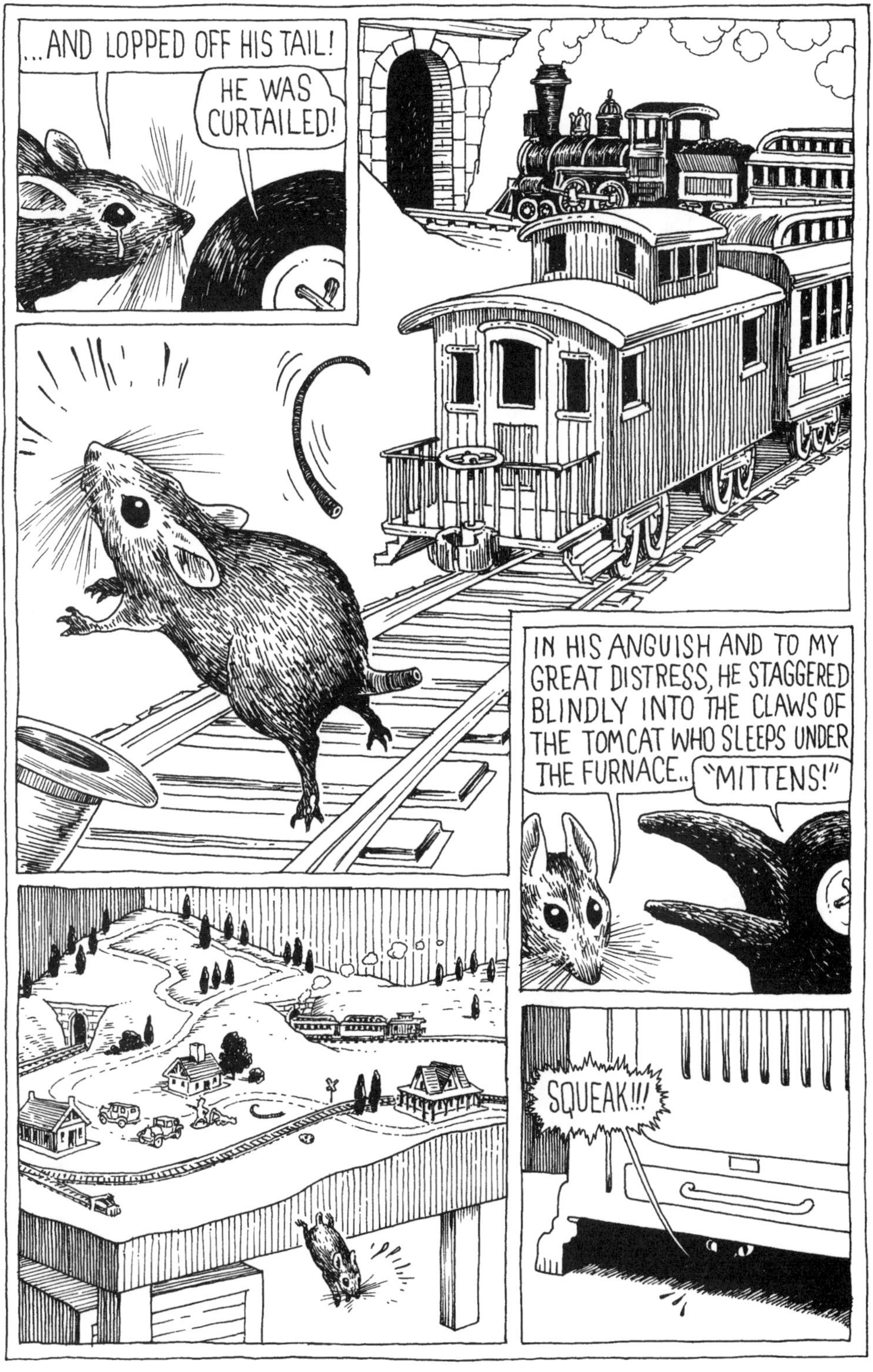
...AND LOPPED OFF HIS TAIL!
HE WAS CURTAILED!
IN HIS ANGUISH AND TO MY GREAT DISTRESS, HE STAGGERED BLINDLY INTO THE CLAWS OF THE TOMCAT WHO SLEEPS UNDER THE FURNACE..
"MITTENS!"
SQUEAK!!!

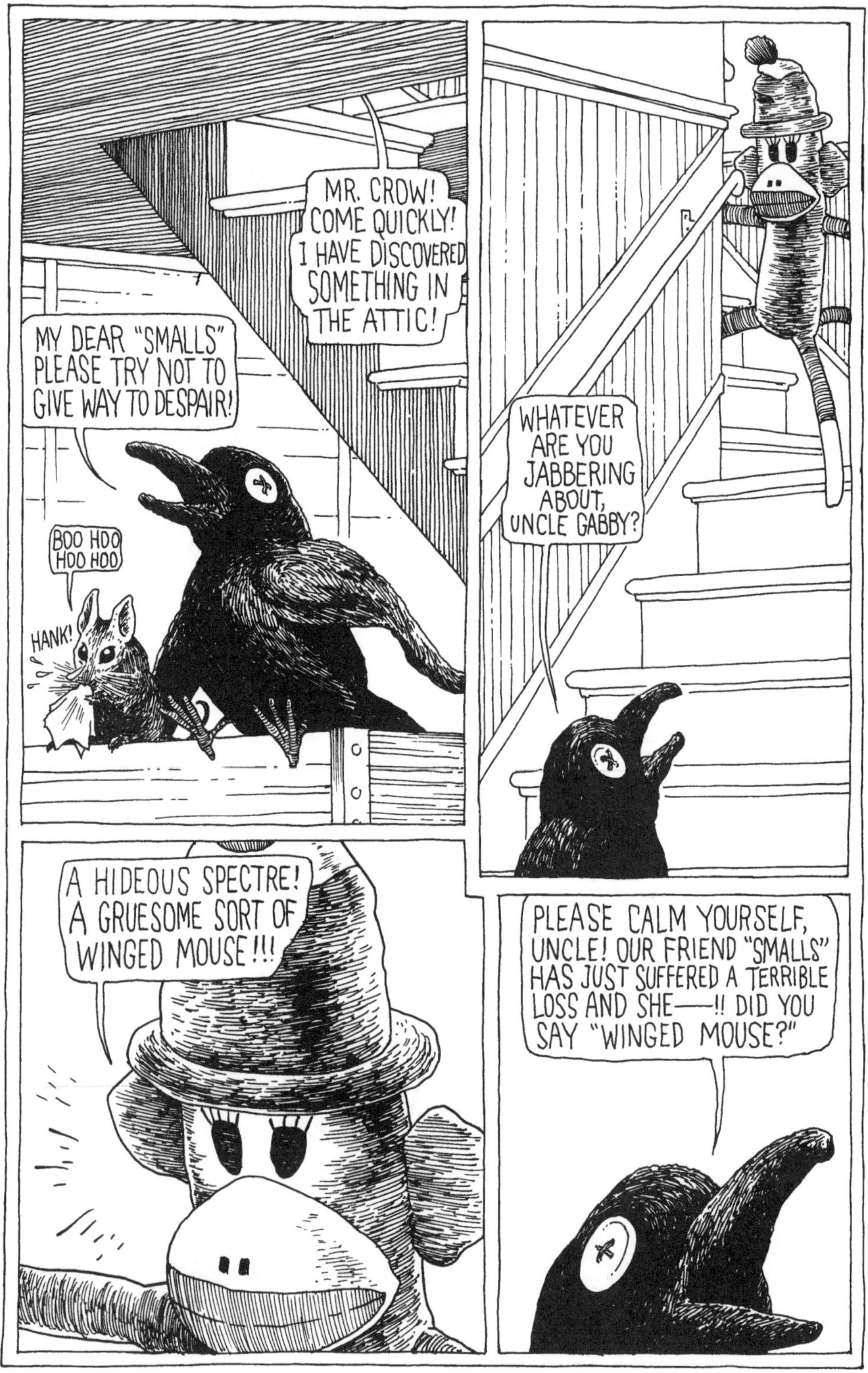
MR. CROW! COME QUICKLY! I HAVE DISCOVERED SOMETHING IN THE ATTIC!
MY DEAR "SMALLS" PLEASE TRY NOT TO GIVE WAY TO DESPAIR!
BOO HOO HOO HOO
HANK!
WHATEVER ARE YOU JABBERING ABOUT, UNCLE GABBY?
A HIDEOUS SPECTRE! A GRUESOME SORT OF WINGED MOUSE!!!
PLEASE CALM YOURSELF, UNCLE! OUR FRIEND "SMALLS" HAS JUST SUFFERED A TERRIBLE LOSS AND SHE——!! DID YOU SAY "WINGED MOUSE?"

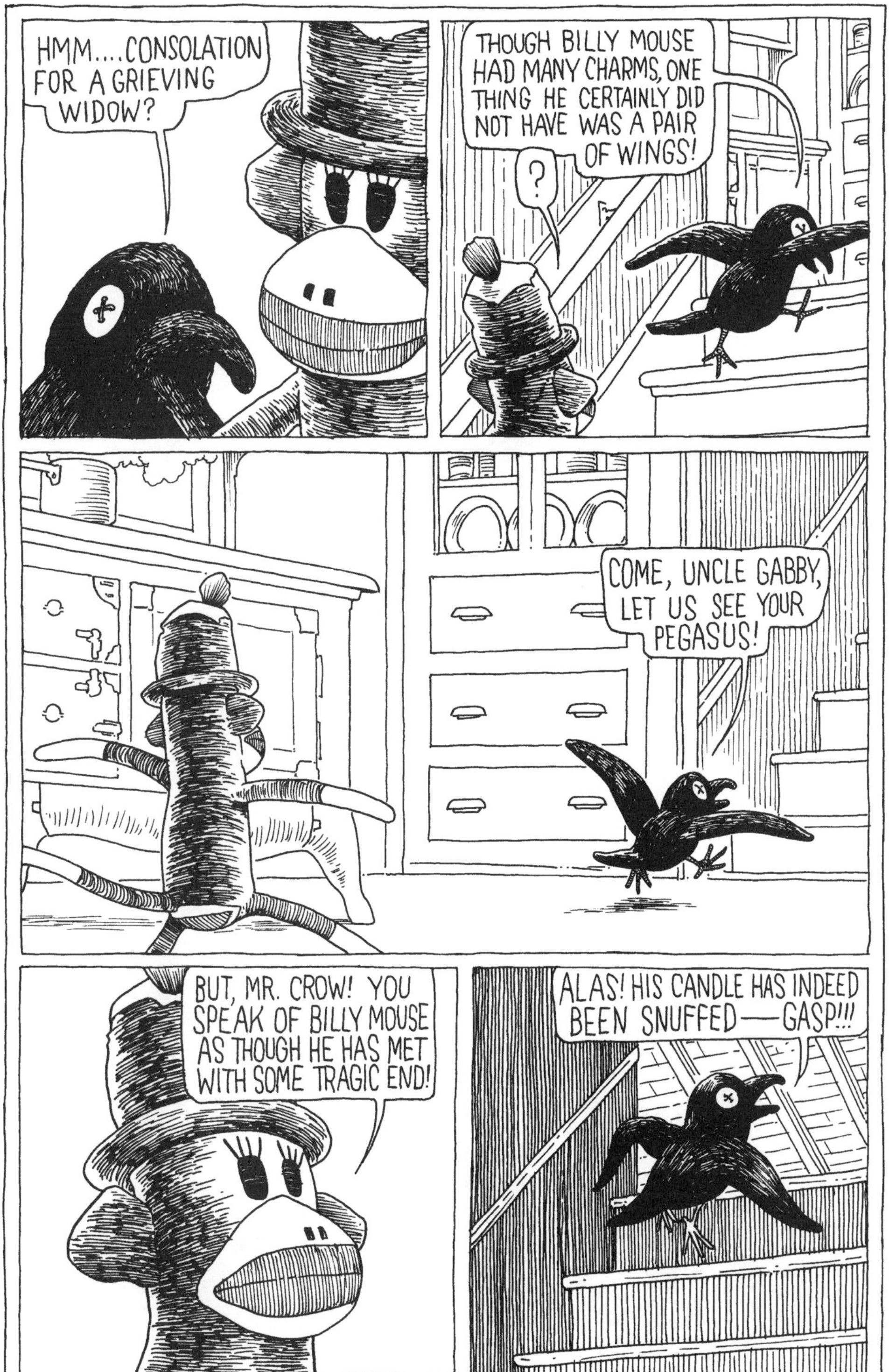
HMM....CONSOLATION FOR A GRIEVING WIDOW?
THOUGH BILLY MOUSE HAD MANY CHARMS, ONE THING HE CERTAINLY DID NOT HAVE WAS A PAIR OF WINGS!
?
COME, UNCLE GABBY, LET US SEE YOUR PEGASUS!
BUT, MR. CROW! YOU SPEAK OF BILLY MOUSE AS THOUGH HE HAS MET WITH SOME TRAGIC END!
ALAS! HIS CANDLE HAS INDEED BEEN SNUFFED——GASP!!!

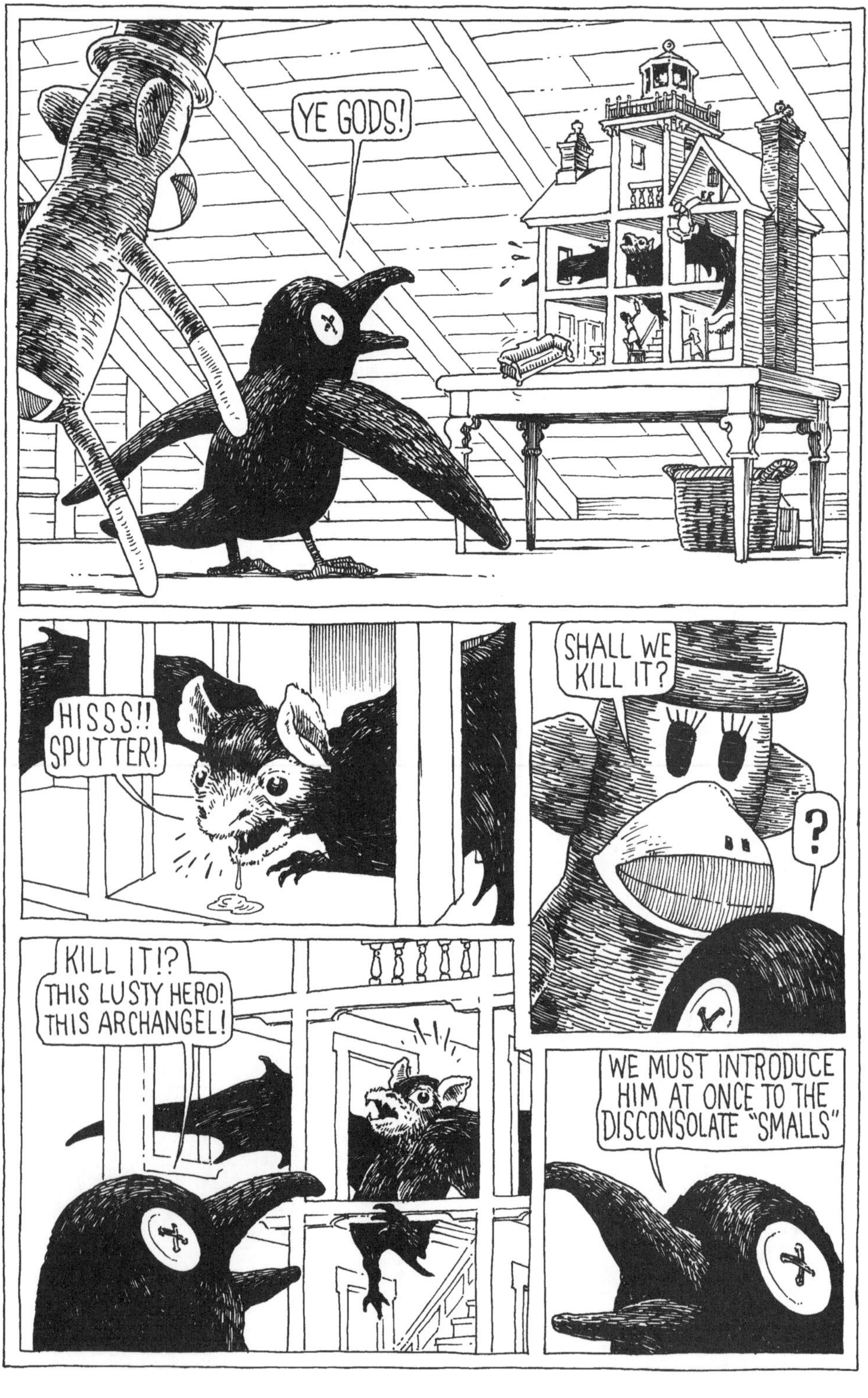
YE GODS!
HISSS!! SPUTTER!
SHALL WE KILL IT?
?
KILL IT!? THIS LUSTY HERO! THIS ARCHANGEL!
WE MUST INTRODUCE HIM AT ONCE TO THE DISCONSOLATE "SMALLS"

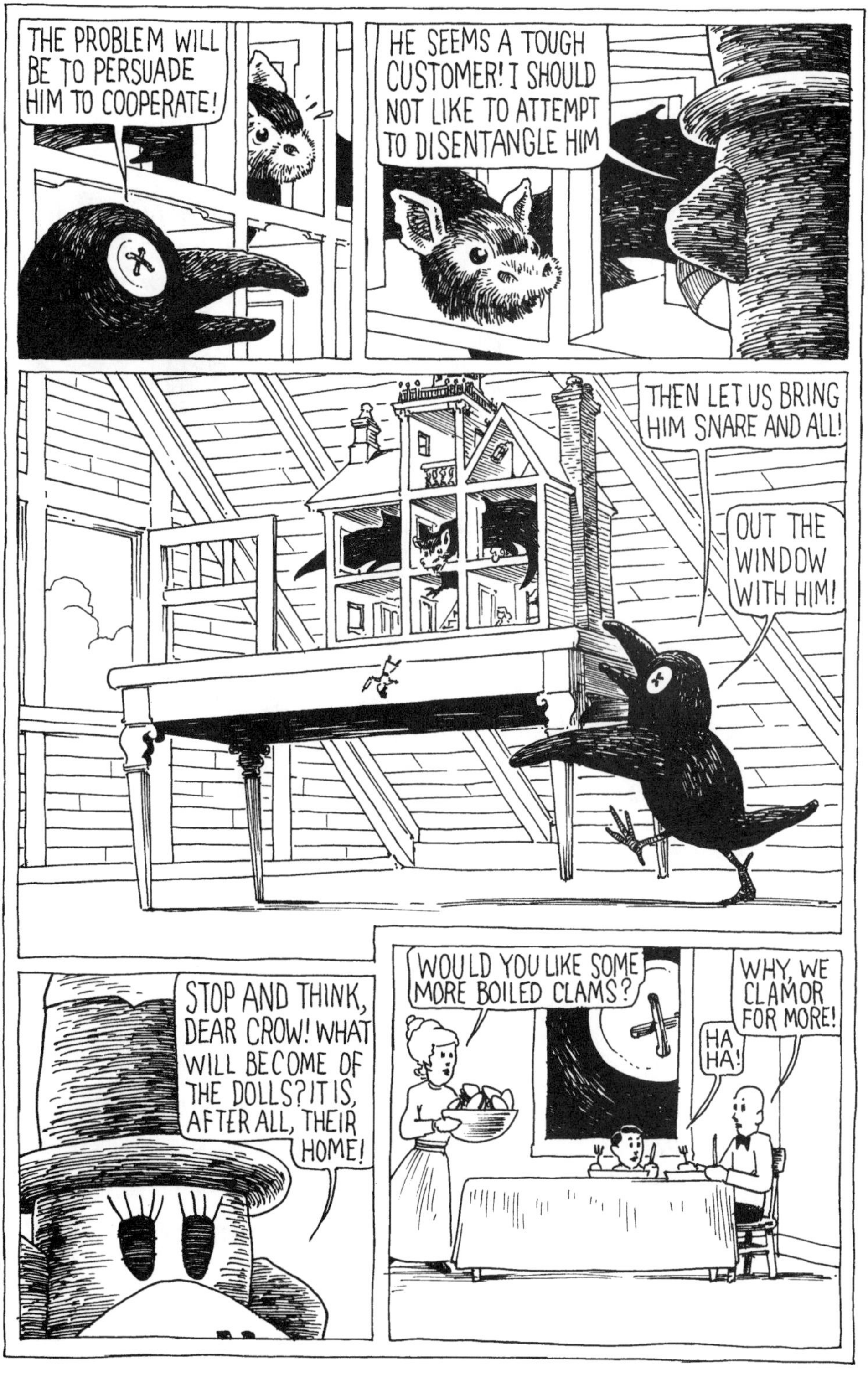
THE PROBLEM WILL BE TO PERSUADE HIM TO COOPERATE!
HE SEEMS A TOUGH CUSTOMER! I SHOULD NOT LIKE TO ATTEMPT TO DISENTANGLE HIM
THEN LET US BRING HIM SNARE AND ALL!
OUT THE WINDOW WITH HIM!
STOP AND THINK, DEAR CROW! WHAT WILL BECOME OF THE DOLLS? IT IS, AFTER ALL, THEIR HOME!
WOULD YOU LIKE SOME MORE BOILED CLAMS?
HA HA!
WHY, WE CLAMOR FOR MORE!

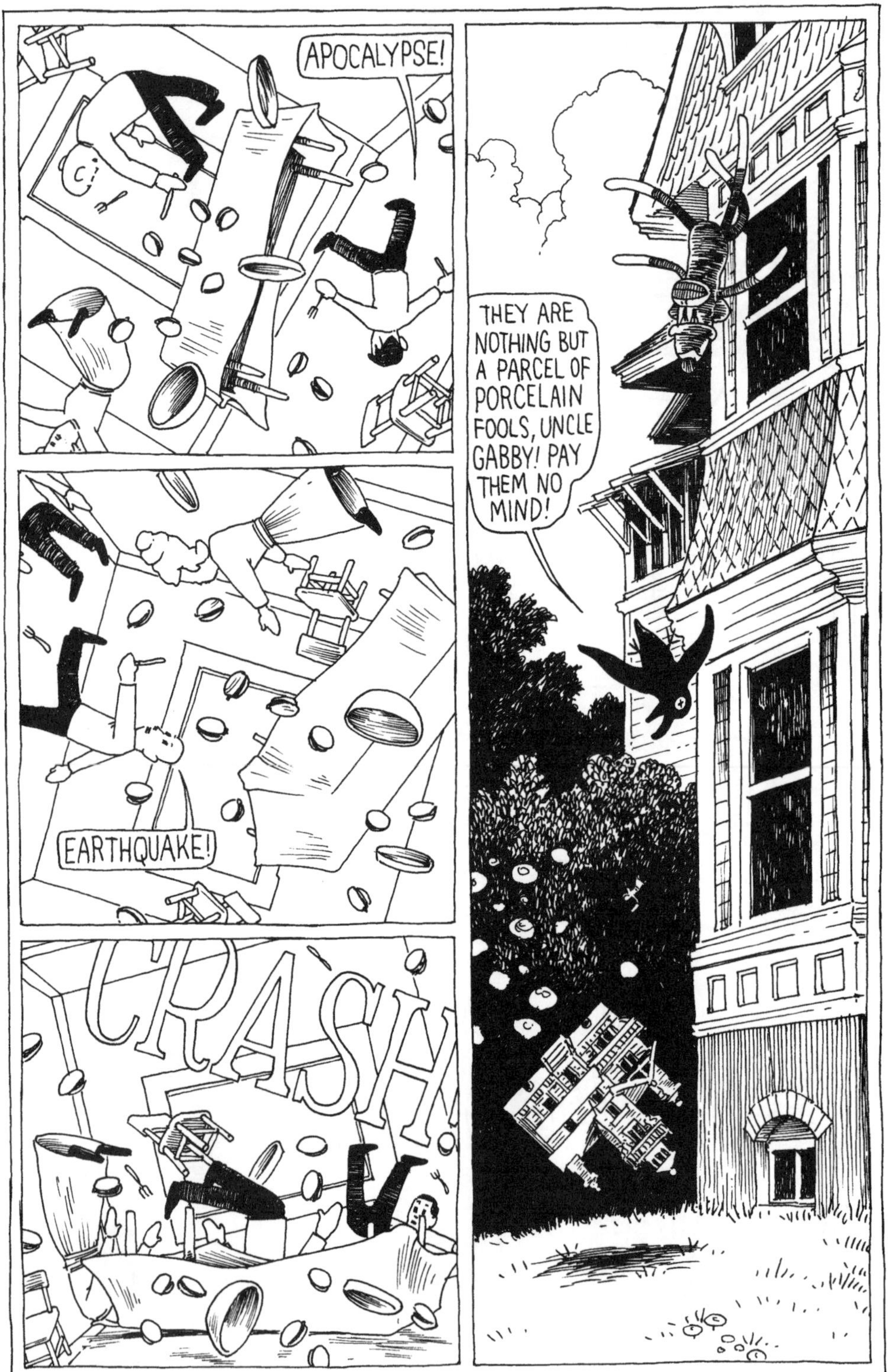
APOCALYPSE!
EARTHQUAKE!
CRASH!
THEY ARE NOTHING BUT A PARCEL OF PORCELAIN FOOLS, UNCLE GABBY! PAY THEM NO MIND!

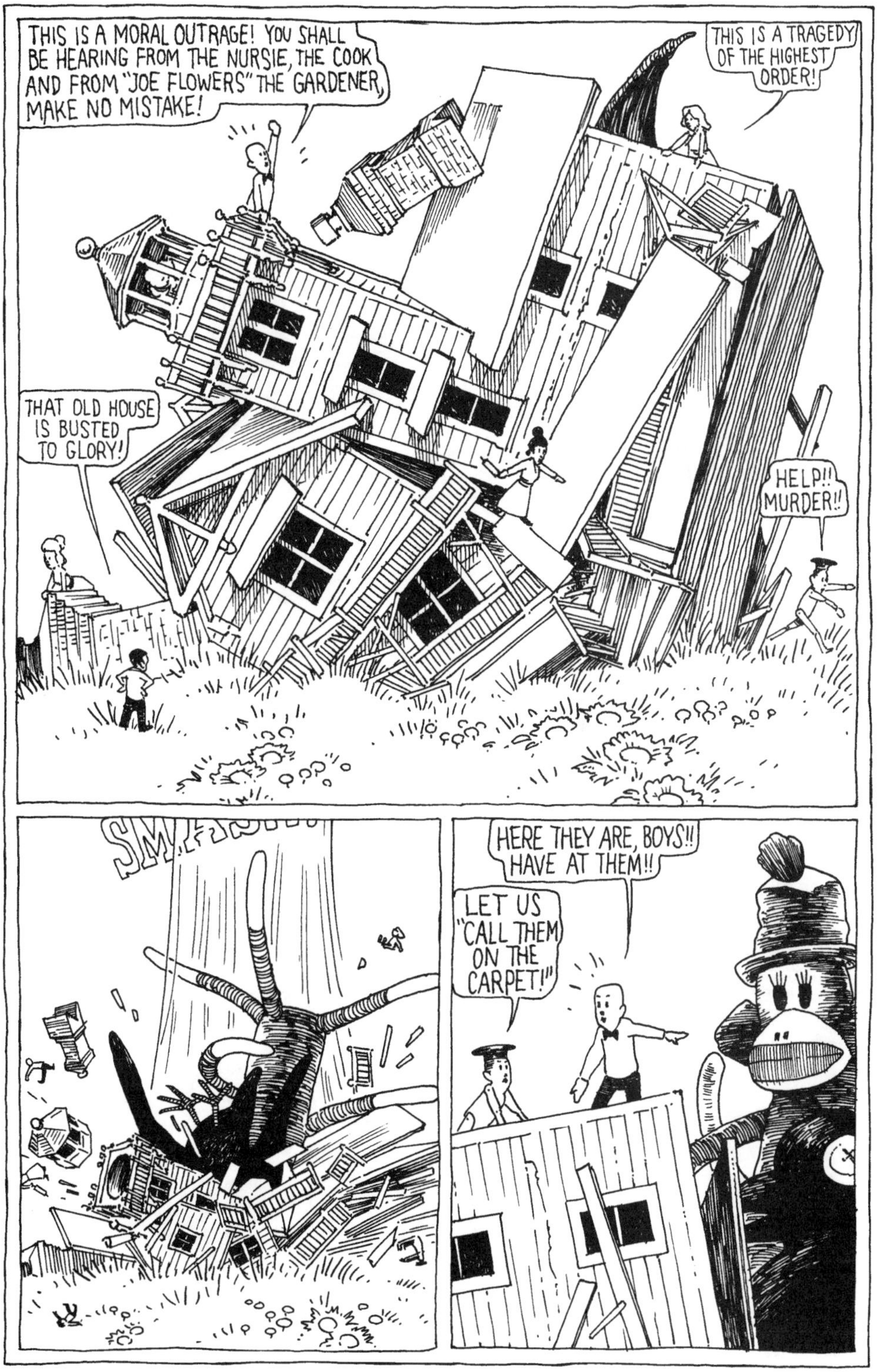

THIS IS A MORAL OUTRAGE! YOU SHALL BE HEARING FROM THE NURSIE, THE COOK AND FROM "JOE FLOWERS" THE GARDENER, MAKE NO MISTAKE!
THIS IS A TRAGEDY OF THE HIGHEST ORDER!
THAT OLD HOUSE IS BUSTED TO GLORY!
HELP!! MURDER!!
HERE THEY ARE, BOYS!! HAVE AT THEM!!
LET US "CALL THEM ON THE CARPET!"

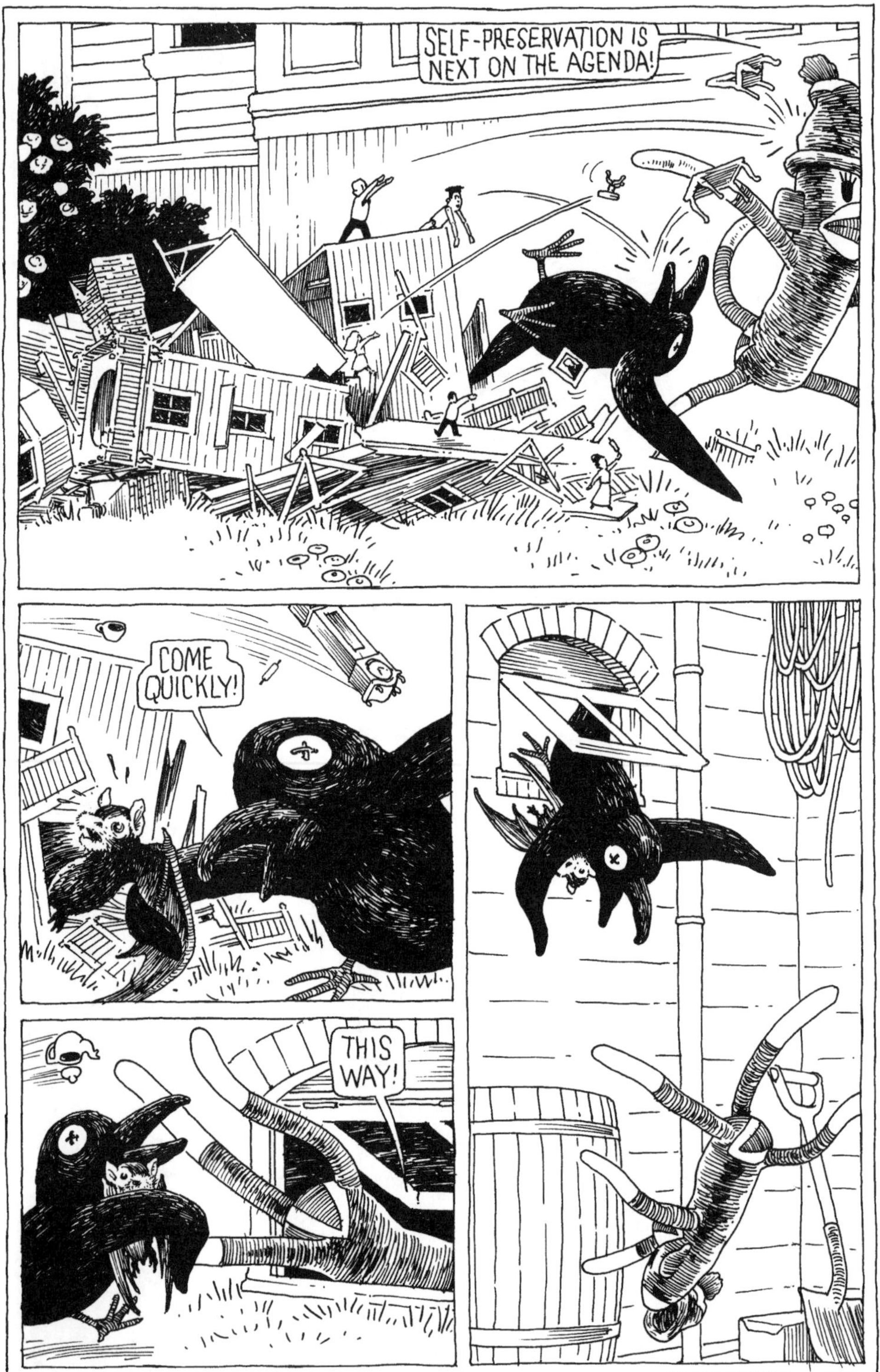
SELF-PRESERVATION IS NEXT ON THE AGENDA!
COME QUICKLY!
THIS WAY!

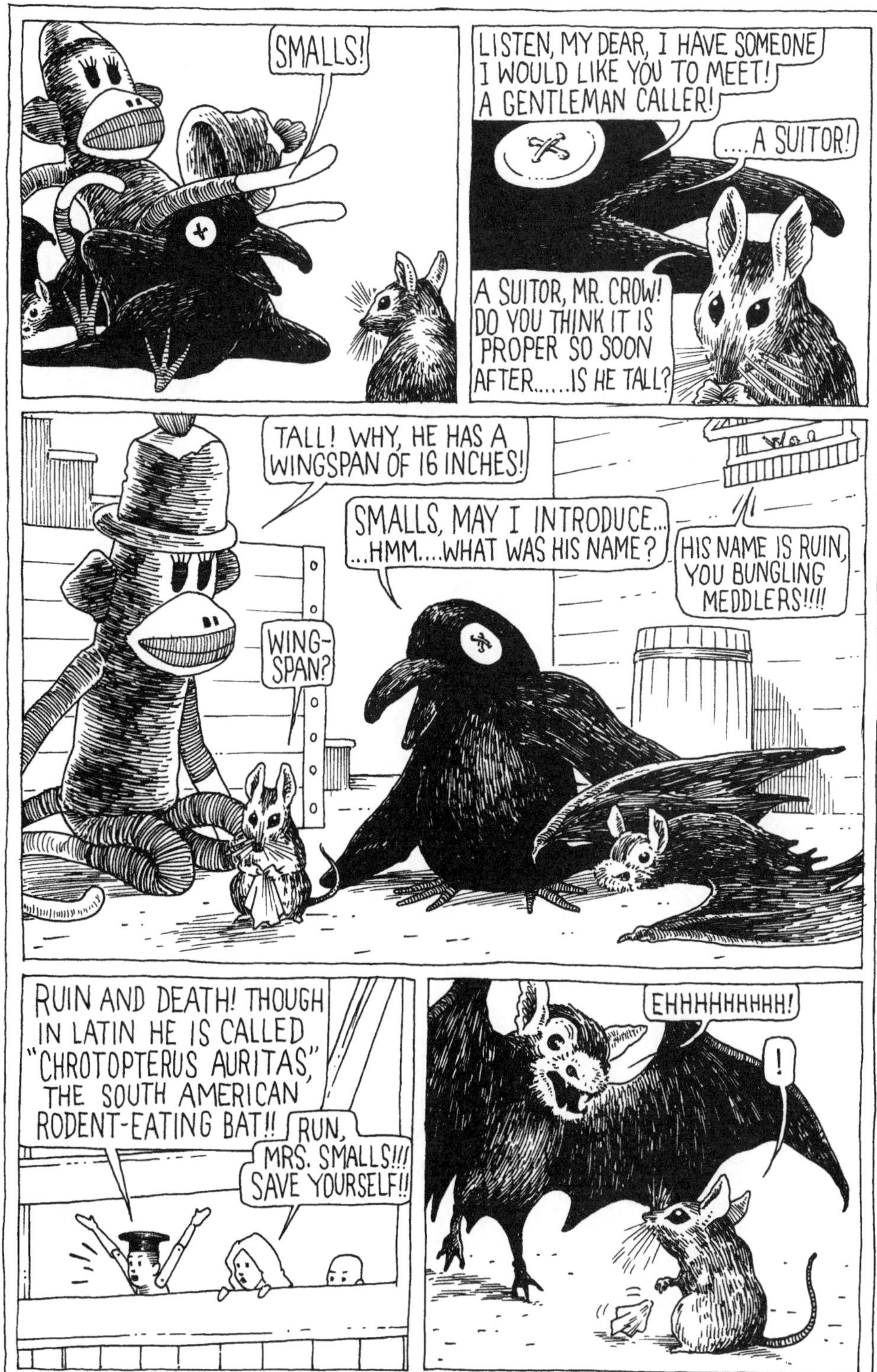
SMALLS!
LISTEN, MY DEAR, I HAVE SOMEONE I WOULD LIKE YOU TO MEET! A GENTLEMAN CALLER!
....A SUITOR!
A SUITOR, MR. CROW! DO YOU THINK IT IS PROPER SO SOON AFTER......IS HE TALL?
TALL! WHY, HE HAS A WINGSPAN OF 16 INCHES!
WING-SPAN?
SMALLS, MAY I INTRODUCE... ...HMM....WHAT WAS HIS NAME?
HIS NAME IS RUIN, YOU BUNGLING MEDDLERS!!!!
RUIN AND DEATH! THOUGH IN LATIN HE IS CALLED "CHROTOPTERUS AURITAS," THE SOUTH AMERICAN RODENT-EATING BAT!!
RUN, MRS. SMALLS!!! SAVE YOURSELF!!
EHHHHHHHHH!
!

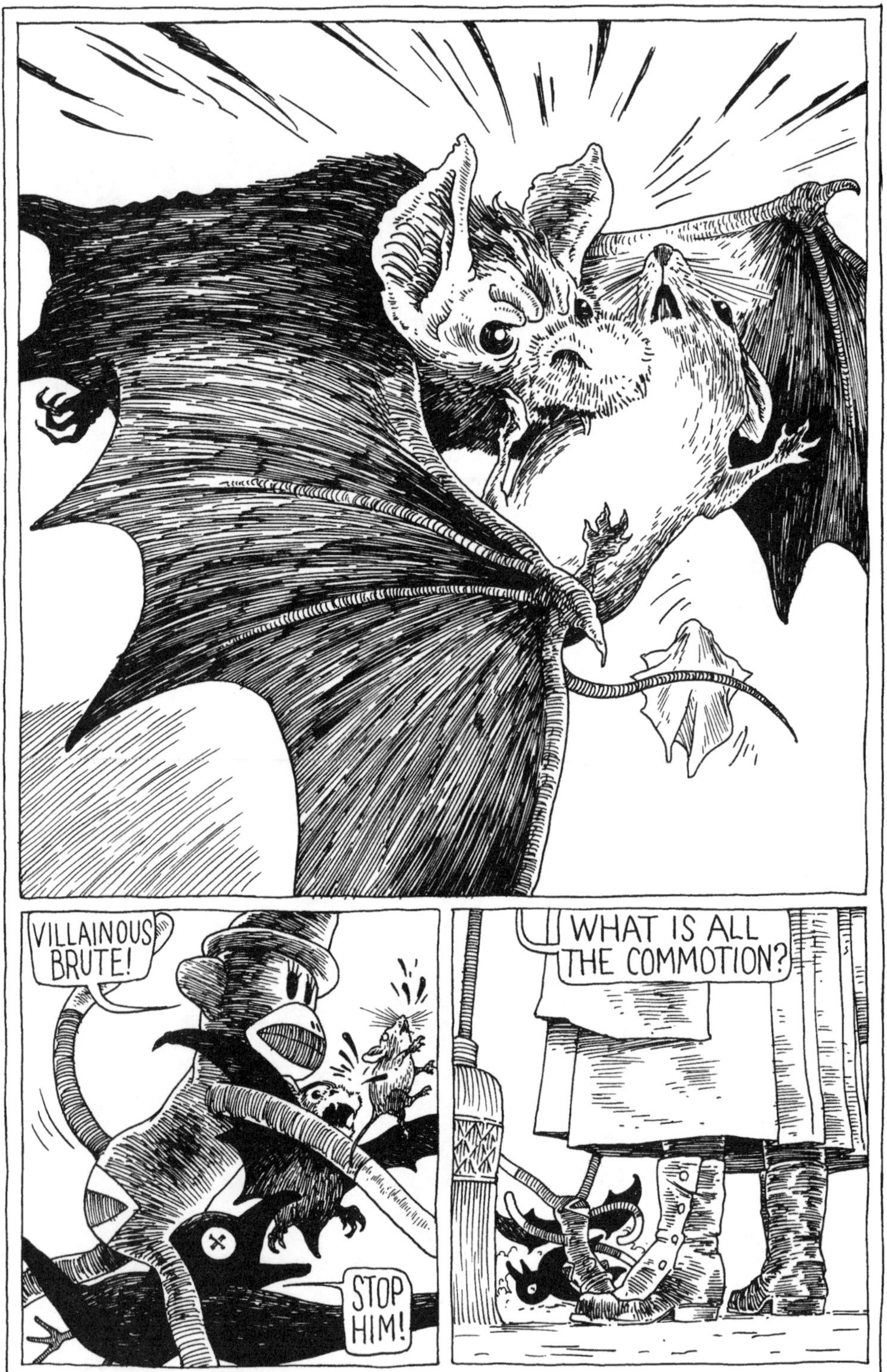
VILLAINOUS BRUTE!
STOP HIM!
WHAT IS ALL THE COMMOTION?

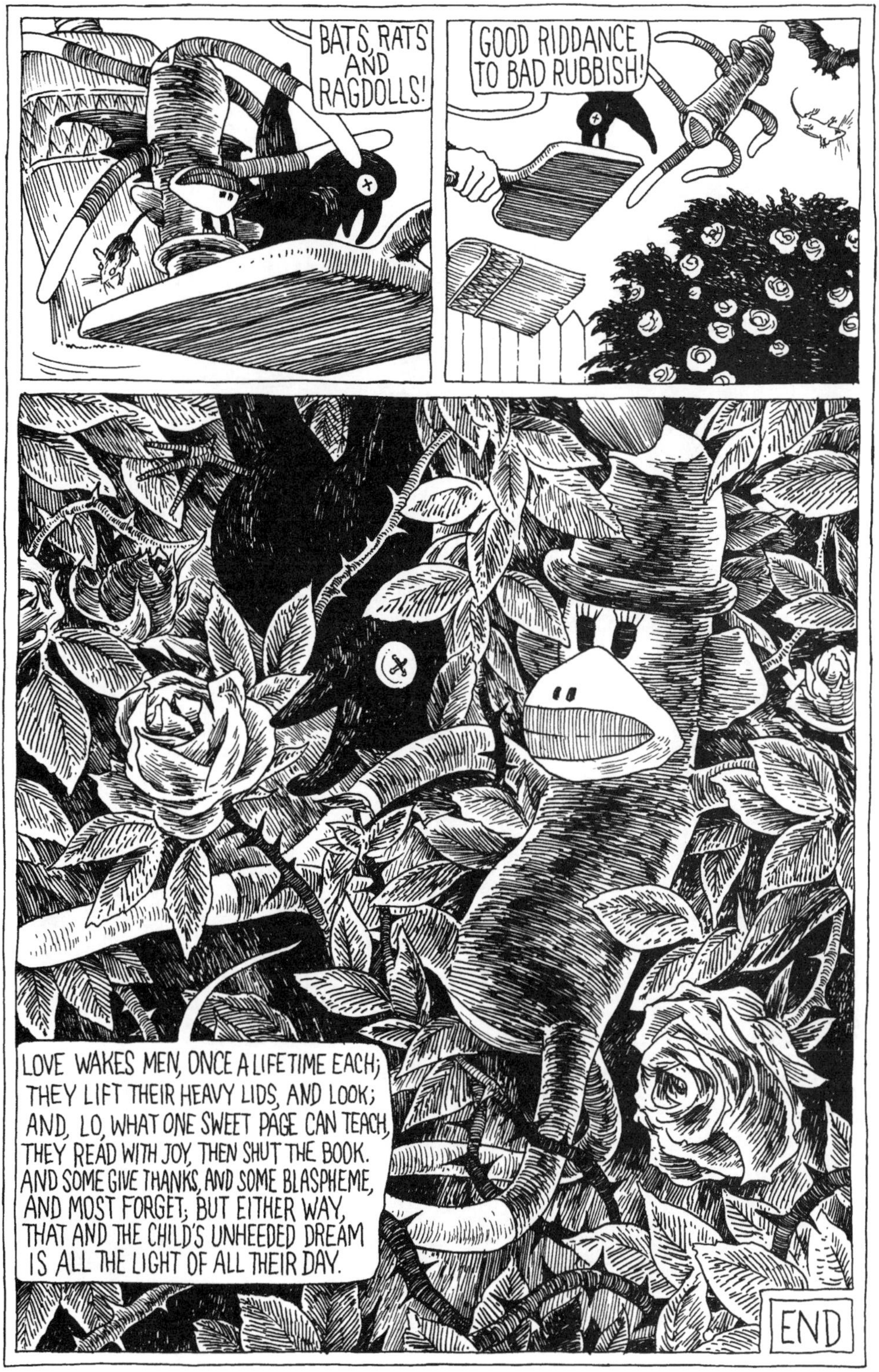
BATS, RATS AND RAGDOLLS!
GOOD RIDDANCE TO BAD RUBBISH!
LOVE WAKES MEN, ONCE A LIFETIME EACH;
THEY LIFT THEIR HEAVY LIDS, AND LOOK;
AND, LO, WHAT ONE SWEET PAGE CAN TEACH,
THEY READ WITH JOY, THEN SHUT THE BOOK.
AND SOME GIVE THANKS, AND SOME BLASPHEME,
AND MOST FORGET; BUT EITHER WAY,
THAT AND THE CHILD'S UNHEEDED DREAM
IS ALL THE LIGHT OF ALL THEIR DAY.
END

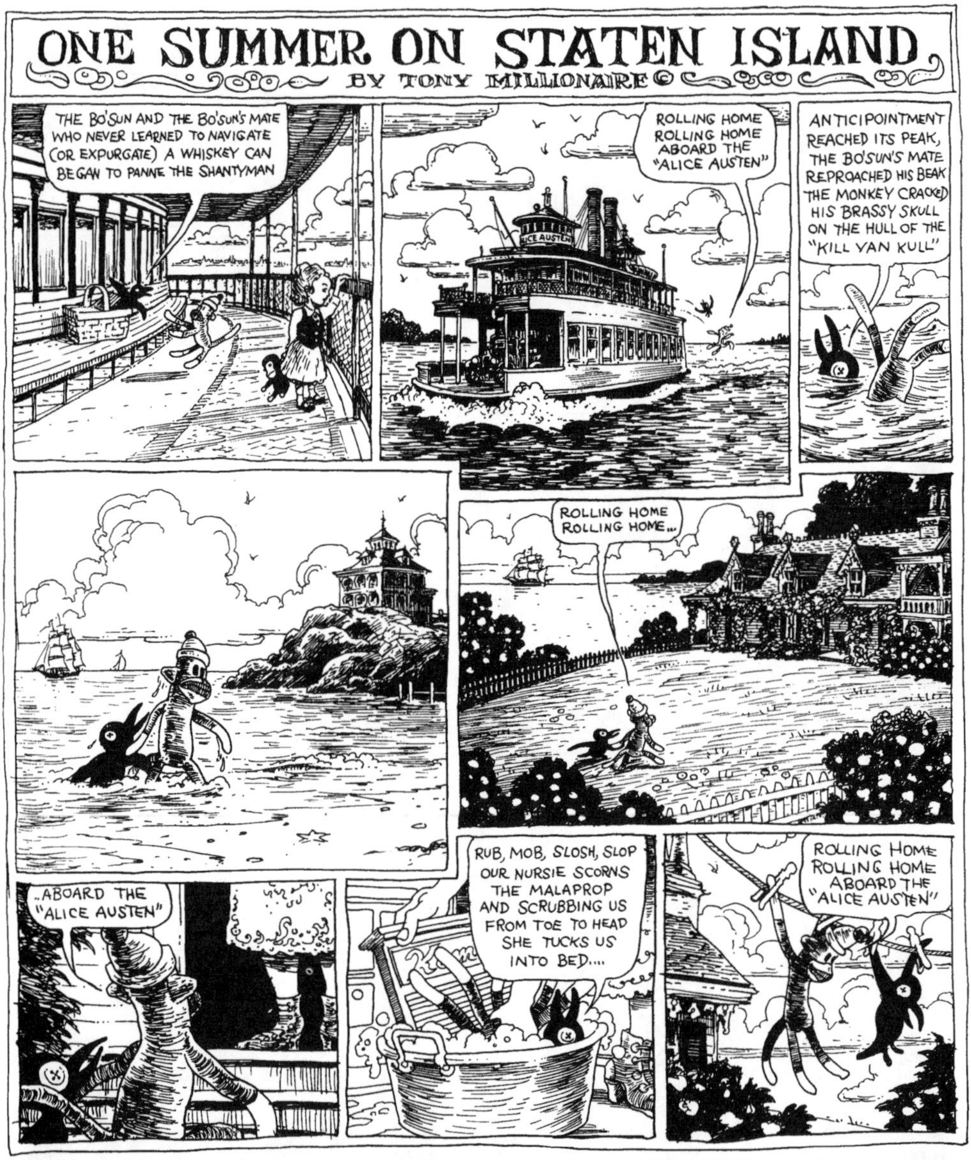
ONE SUMMER ON STATEN ISLAND
BY TONY MILLIONAIRE©
THE BO'SUN AND THE BO'SUN'S MATE WHO NEVER LEARNED TO NAVIGATE (OR EXPURGATE) A WHISKEY CAN BEGAN TO PANNE THE SHANTYMAN
ROLLING HOME ROLLING HOME ABOARD THE "ALICE AUSTEN"
ANTICIPOINTMENT REACHED ITS PEAK, THE BO'SUN'S MATE REPROACHED HIS BEAK THE MONKEY CRACKED HIS BRASSY SKULL ON THE HULL OF THE "KILL VAN KULL"
ROLLING HOME ROLLING HOME...
...ABOARD THE "ALICE AUSTEN"
RUB, MOB, SLOSH, SLOP OUR NURSIE SCORNS THE MALAPROP AND SCRUBBING US FROM TOE TO HEAD SHE TUCKS US INTO BED....
ROLLING HOME ROLLING HOME ABOARD THE "ALICE AUSTEN"

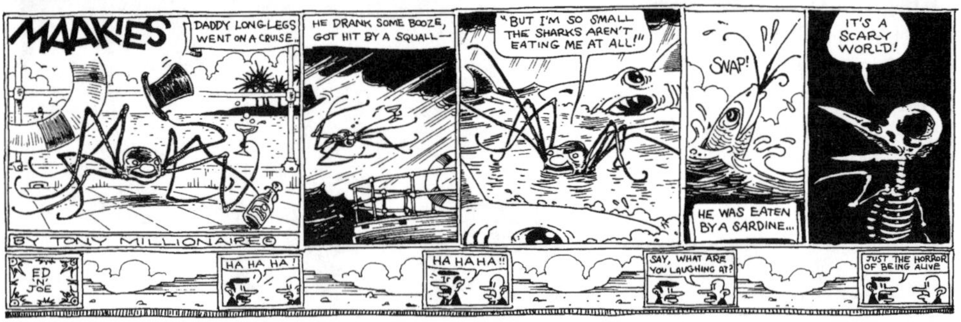
MAAKIES
DADDY LONG-LEGS WENT ON A CRUISE.
HE DRANK SOME BOOZE, GOT HIT BY A SQUALL—
"BUT I'M SO SMALL THE SHARKS AREN'T EATING ME AT ALL!"
SNAP!
HE WAS EATEN BY A SARDINE...
IT'S A SCARY WORLD!
BY TONY MILLIONAIRE
ED 'N' JOE
HA HA HA!
HA HA HA!!
SAY, WHAT ARE YOU LAUGHING AT?
JUST THE HORROR OF BEING ALIVE

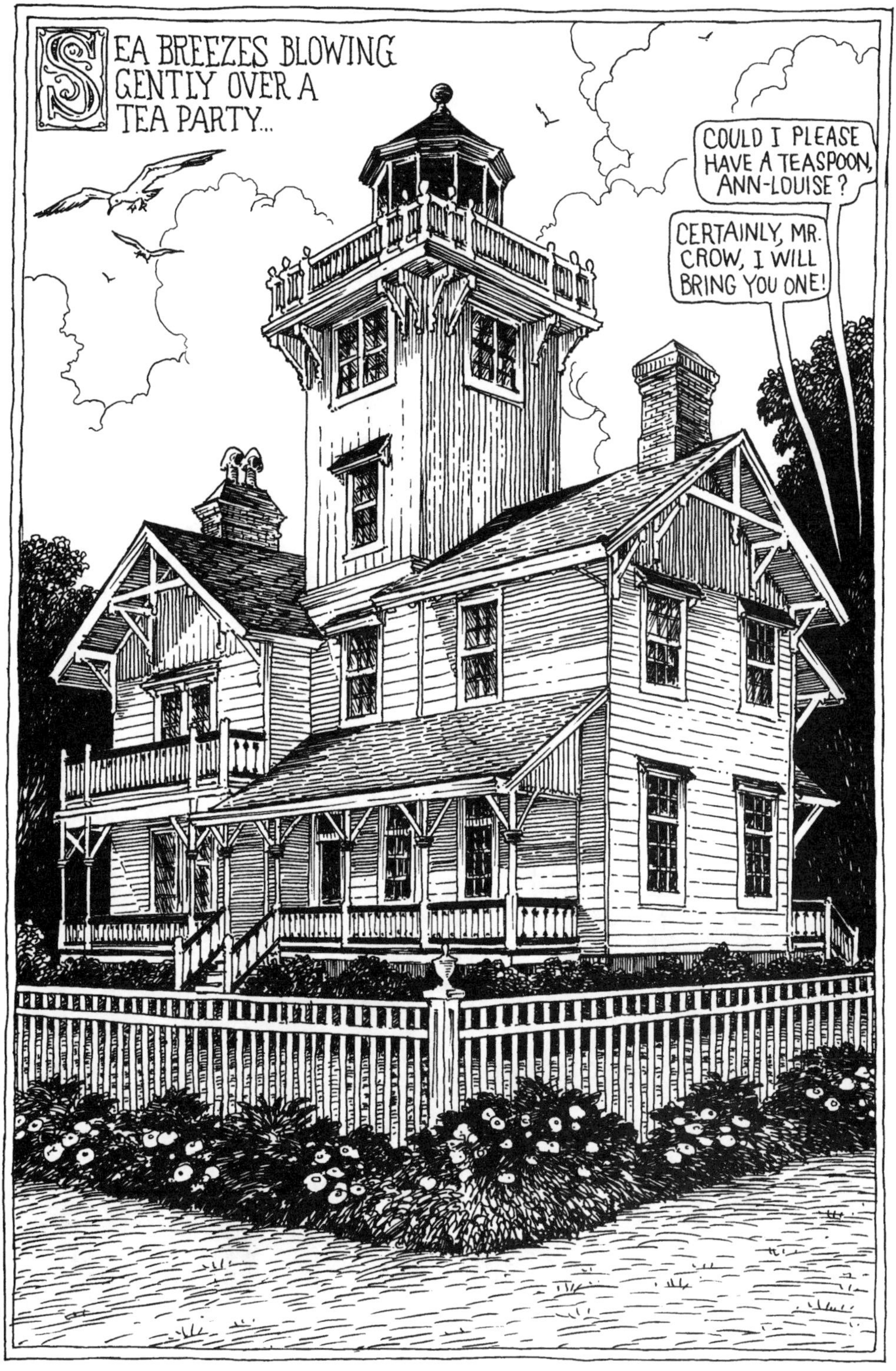
SEA BREEZES BLOWING GENTLY OVER A TEA PARTY...
COULD I PLEASE HAVE A TEASPOON, ANN-LOUISE?
CERTAINLY, MR. CROW, I WILL BRING YOU ONE!

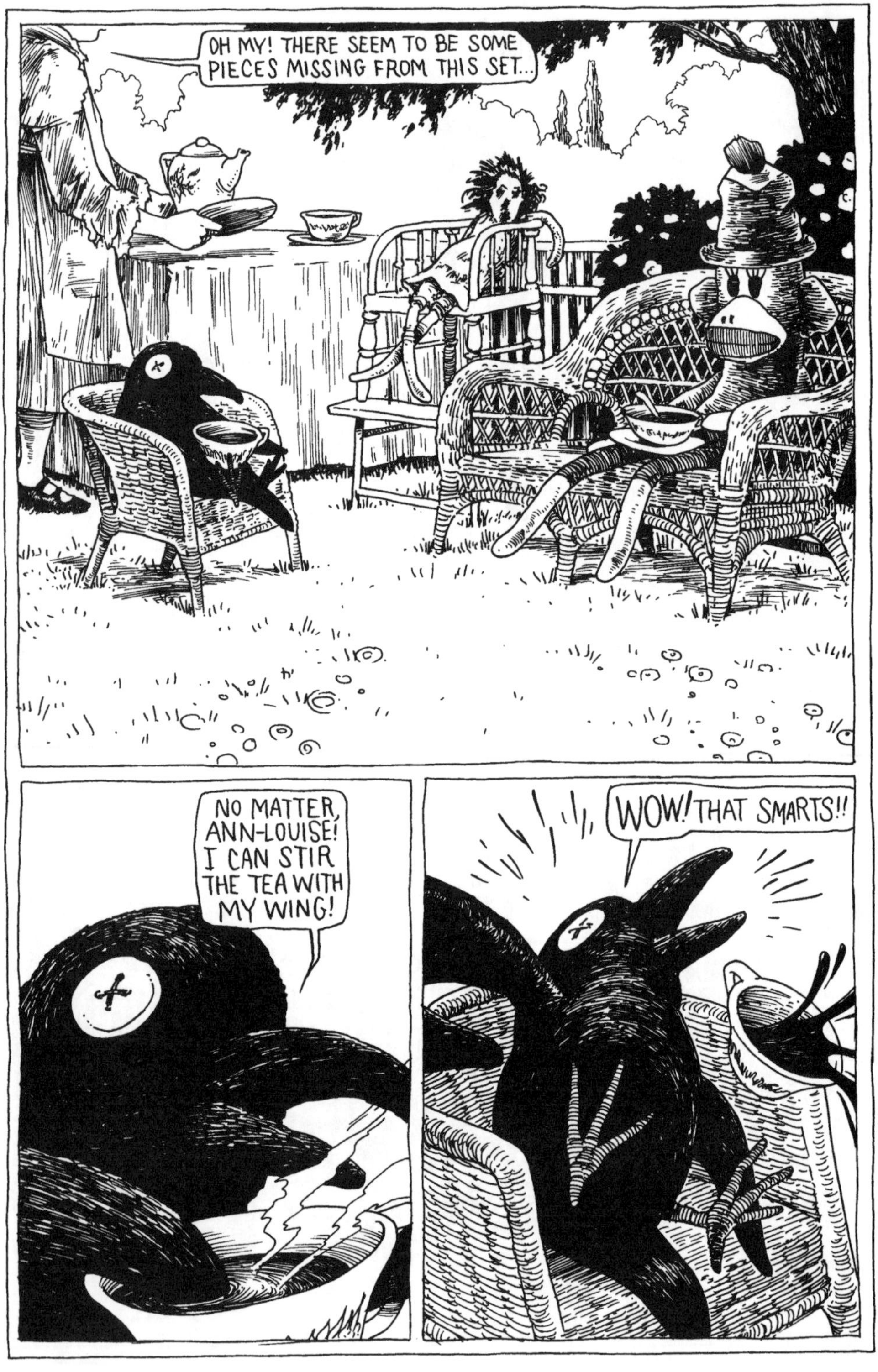
OH MY! THERE SEEM TO BE SOME PIECES MISSING FROM THIS SET...
NO MATTER, ANN-LOUISE! I CAN STIR THE TEA WITH MY WING!
WOW! THAT SMARTS!!

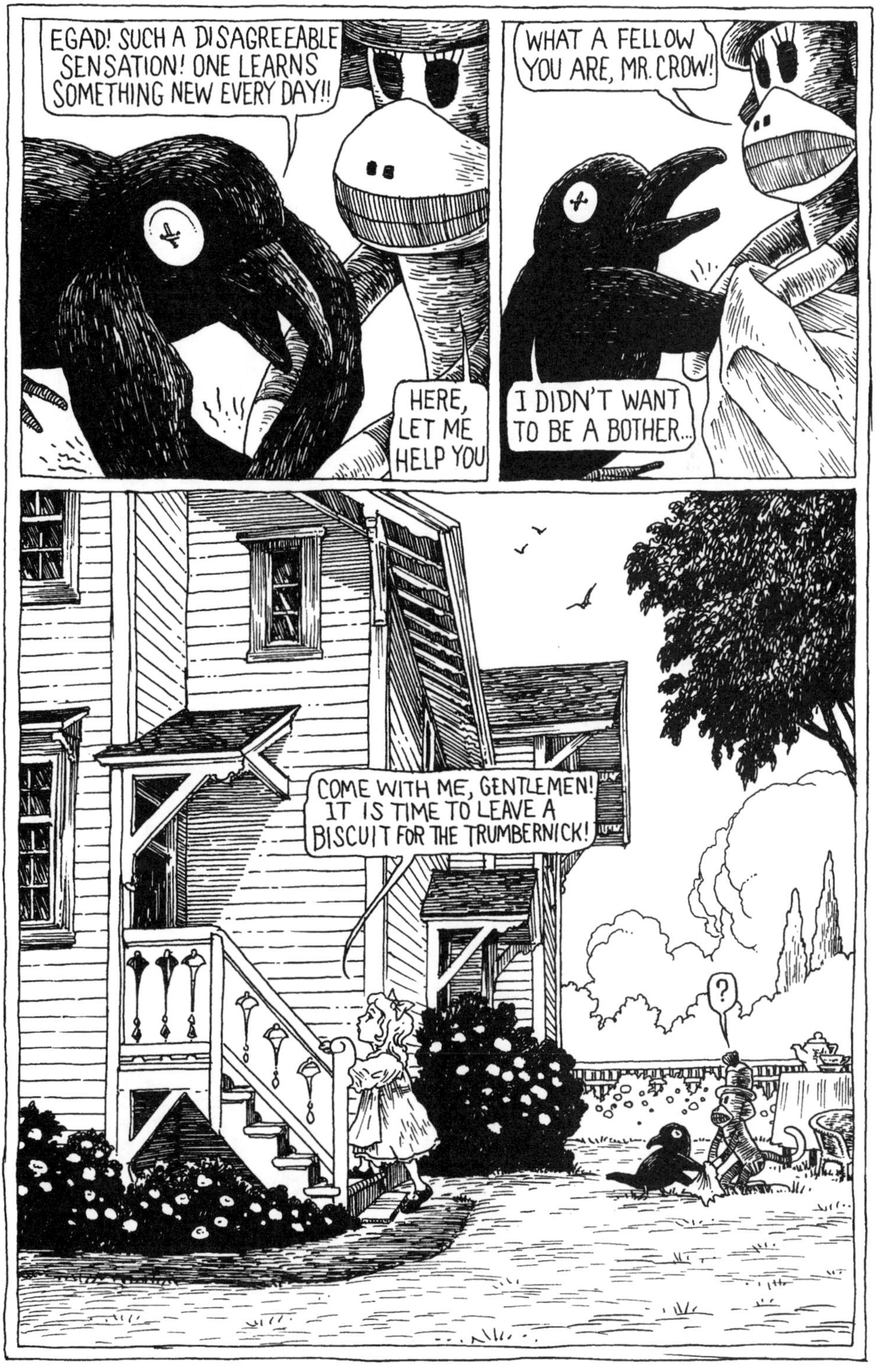
EGAD! SUCH A DISAGREEABLE SENSATION! ONE LEARNS SOMETHING NEW EVERY DAY!!
HERE, LET ME HELP YOU
WHAT A FELLOW YOU ARE, MR. CROW!
I DIDN'T WANT TO BE A BOTHER...
COME WITH ME, GENTLEMEN! IT IS TIME TO LEAVE A BISCUIT FOR THE TRUMBERNICK!
?

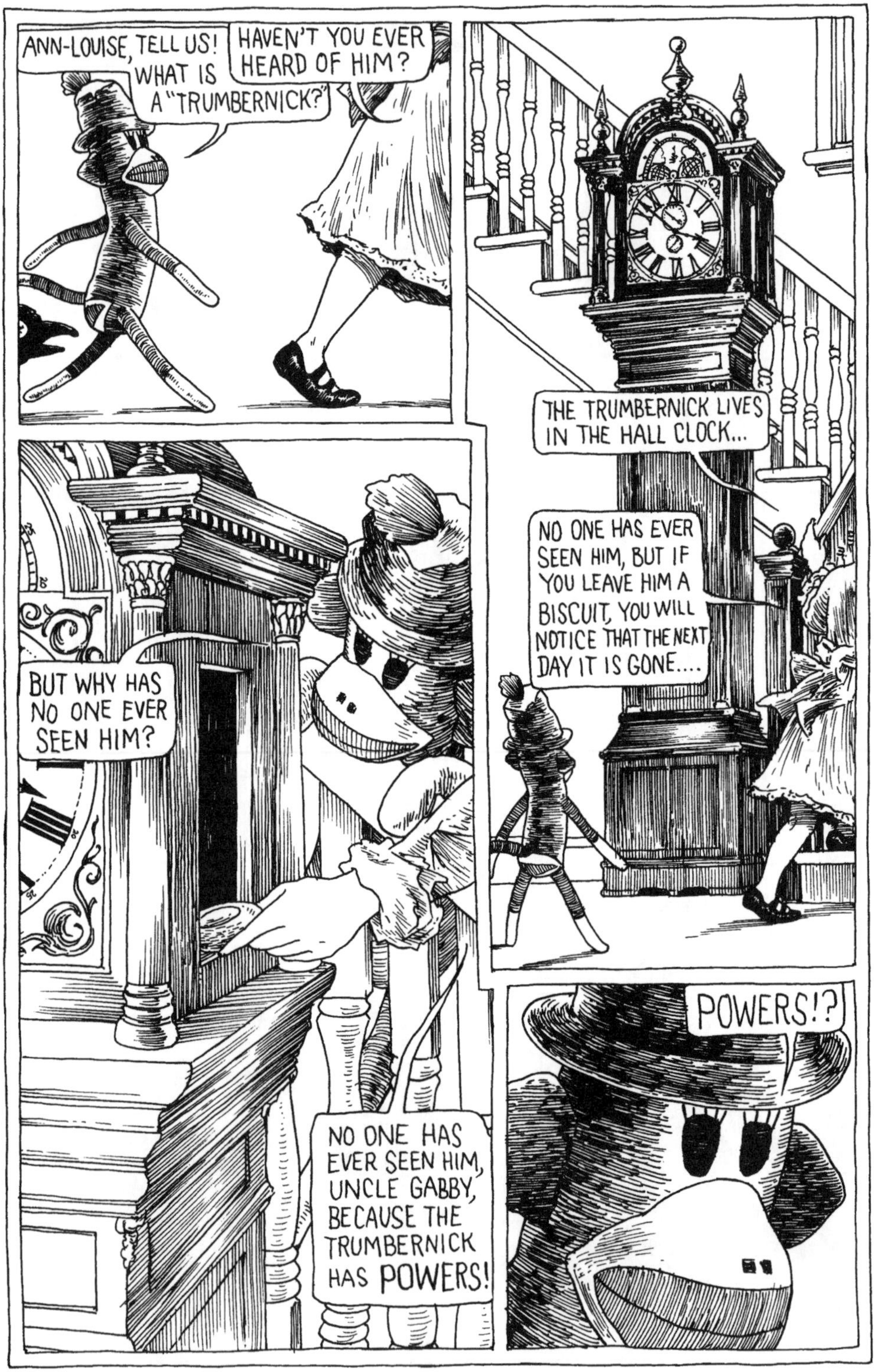
ANN-LOUISE, TELL US! WHAT IS A "TRUMBERNICK?"
HAVEN'T YOU EVER HEARD OF HIM?
THE TRUMBERNICK LIVES IN THE HALL CLOCK...
NO ONE HAS EVER SEEN HIM, BUT IF YOU LEAVE HIM A BISCUIT, YOU WILL NOTICE THAT THE NEXT DAY IT IS GONE....
BUT WHY HAS NO ONE EVER SEEN HIM?
NO ONE HAS EVER SEEN HIM, UNCLE GABBY, BECAUSE THE TRUMBERNICK HAS POWERS!
POWERS!?

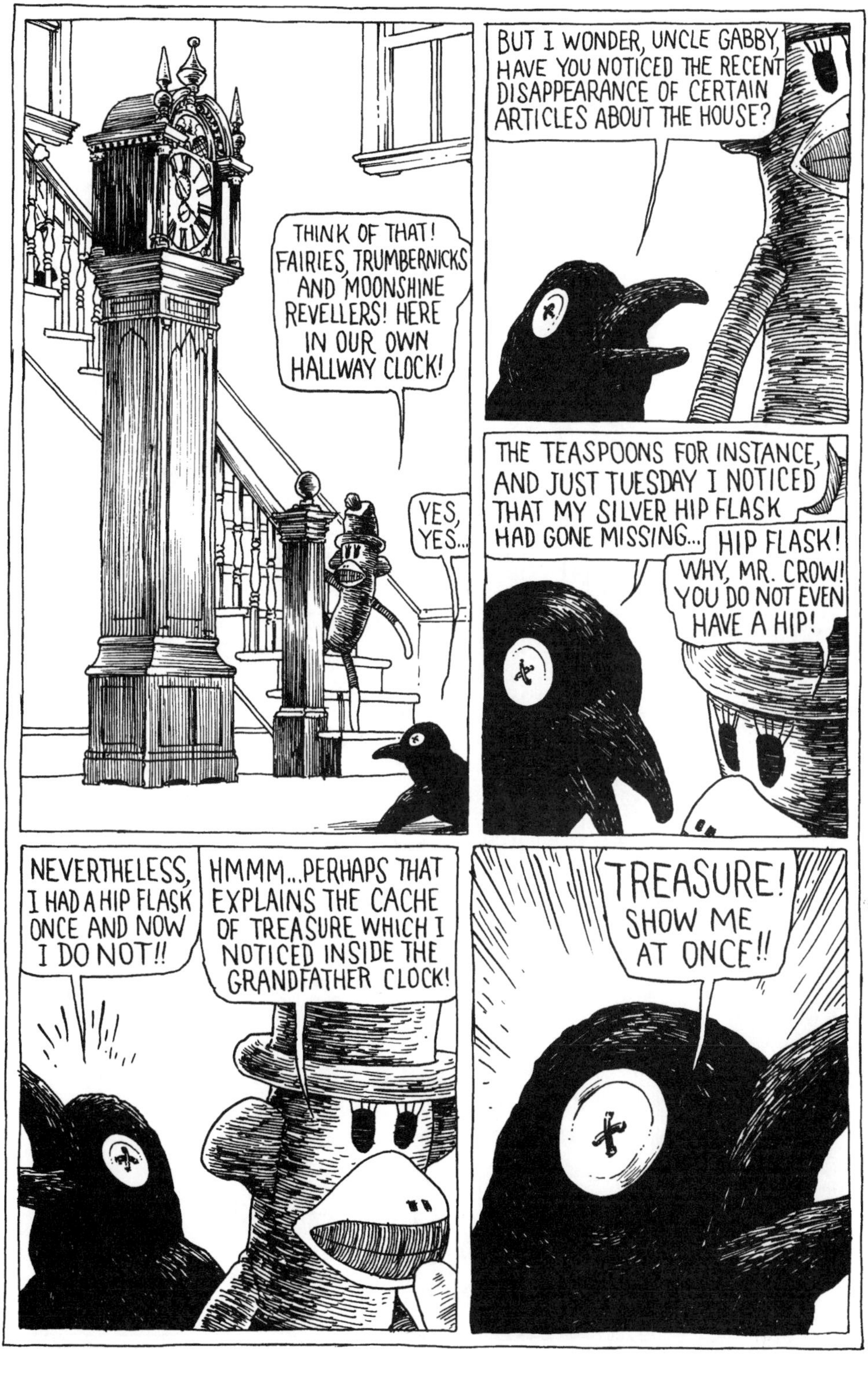
THINK OF THAT! FAIRIES, TRUMBERNICKS AND MOONSHINE REVELLERS! HERE IN OUR OWN HALLWAY CLOCK!
YES, YES...
BUT I WONDER, UNCLE GABBY, HAVE YOU NOTICED THE RECENT DISAPPEARANCE OF CERTAIN ARTICLES ABOUT THE HOUSE?
THE TEASPOONS FOR INSTANCE, AND JUST TUESDAY I NOTICED THAT MY SILVER HIP FLASK HAD GONE MISSING...
HIP FLASK! WHY, MR. CROW! YOU DO NOT EVEN HAVE A HIP!
NEVERTHELESS, I HAD A HIP FLASK ONCE AND NOW I DO NOT!!
HMMM...PERHAPS THAT EXPLAINS THE CACHE OF TREASURE WHICH I NOTICED INSIDE THE GRANDFATHER CLOCK!
TREASURE! SHOW ME AT ONCE!!

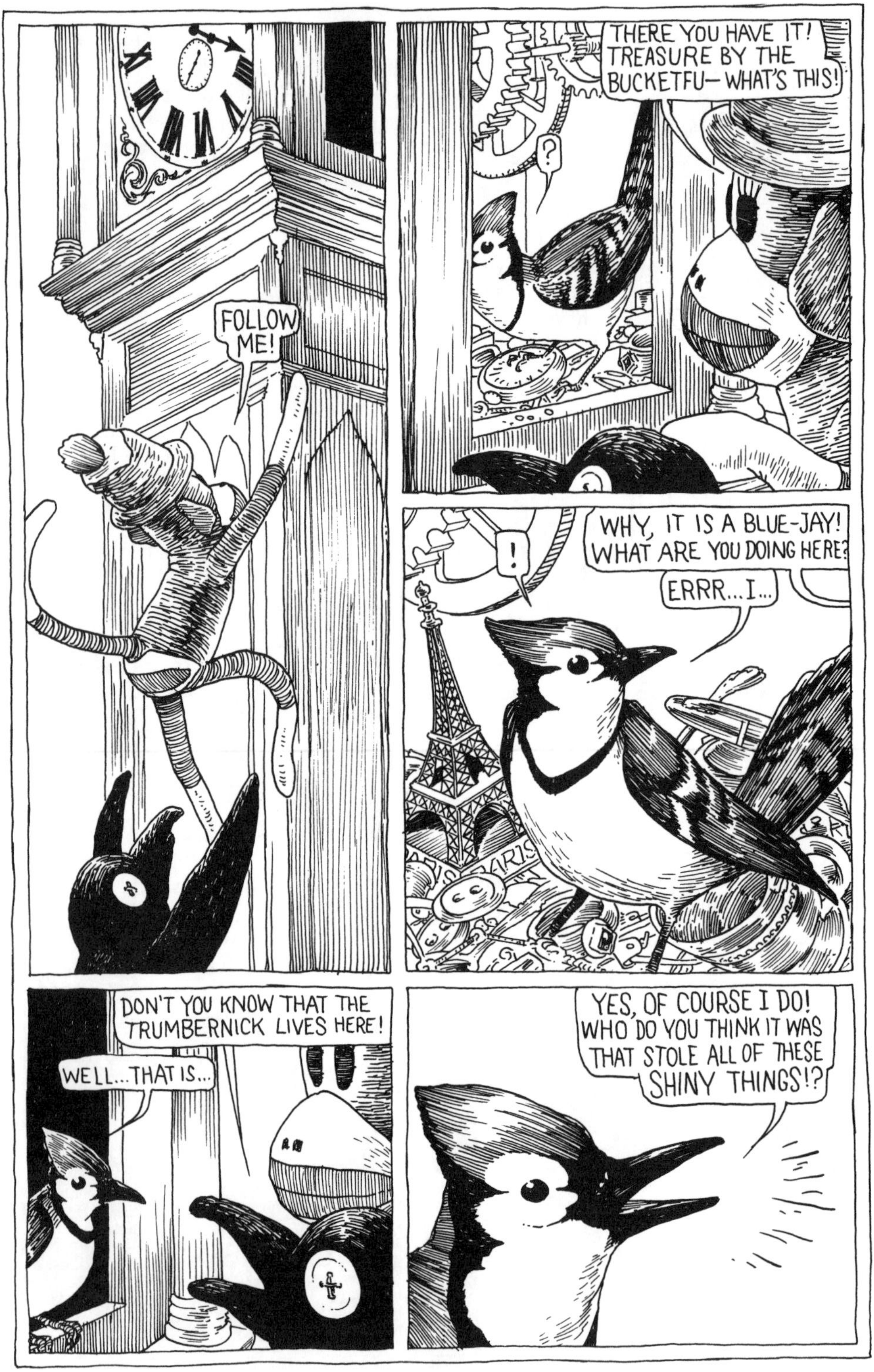
FOLLOW ME!
THERE YOU HAVE IT! TREASURE BY THE BUCKETFU— WHAT'S THIS!
?
!
WHY, IT IS A BLUE-JAY! WHAT ARE YOU DOING HERE?
ERRR... I...
PARIS
DON'T YOU KNOW THAT THE TRUMBERNICK LIVES HERE!
WELL... THAT IS...
YES, OF COURSE I DO! WHO DO YOU THINK IT WAS THAT STOLE ALL OF THESE SHINY THINGS!?

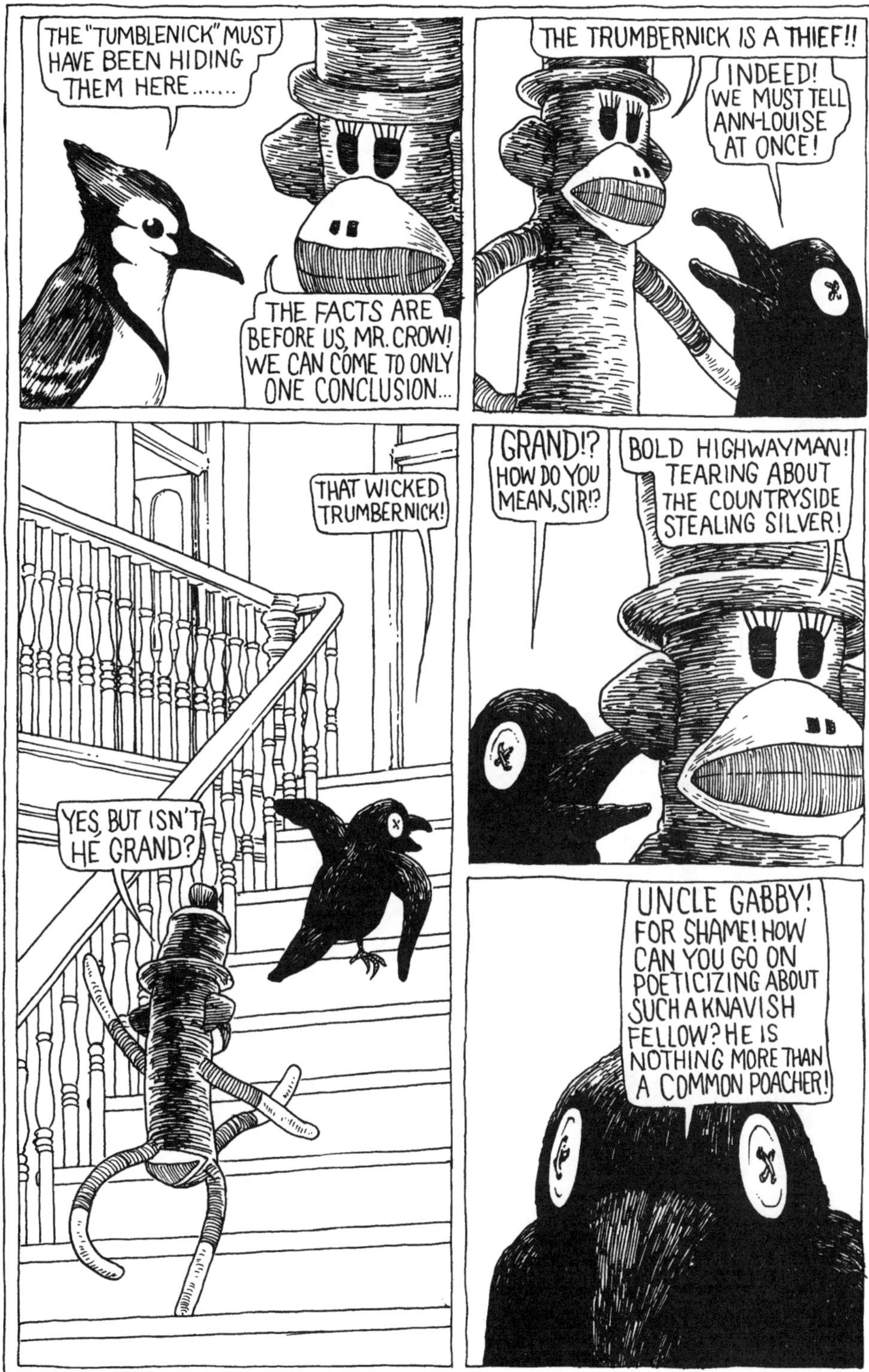
THE "TUMBLENICK" MUST HAVE BEEN HIDING THEM HERE.......
THE FACTS ARE BEFORE US, MR. CROW! WE CAN COME TO ONLY ONE CONCLUSION...
THE TRUMBERNICK IS A THIEF!!
INDEED! WE MUST TELL ANN-LOUISE AT ONCE!
THAT WICKED TRUMBERNICK!
YES, BUT ISN'T HE GRAND?
GRAND!? HOW DO YOU MEAN, SIR!?
BOLD HIGHWAYMAN! TEARING ABOUT THE COUNTRYSIDE STEALING SILVER!
UNCLE GABBY! FOR SHAME! HOW CAN YOU GO ON POETICIZING ABOUT SUCH A KNAVISH FELLOW? HE IS NOTHING MORE THAN A COMMON POACHER!

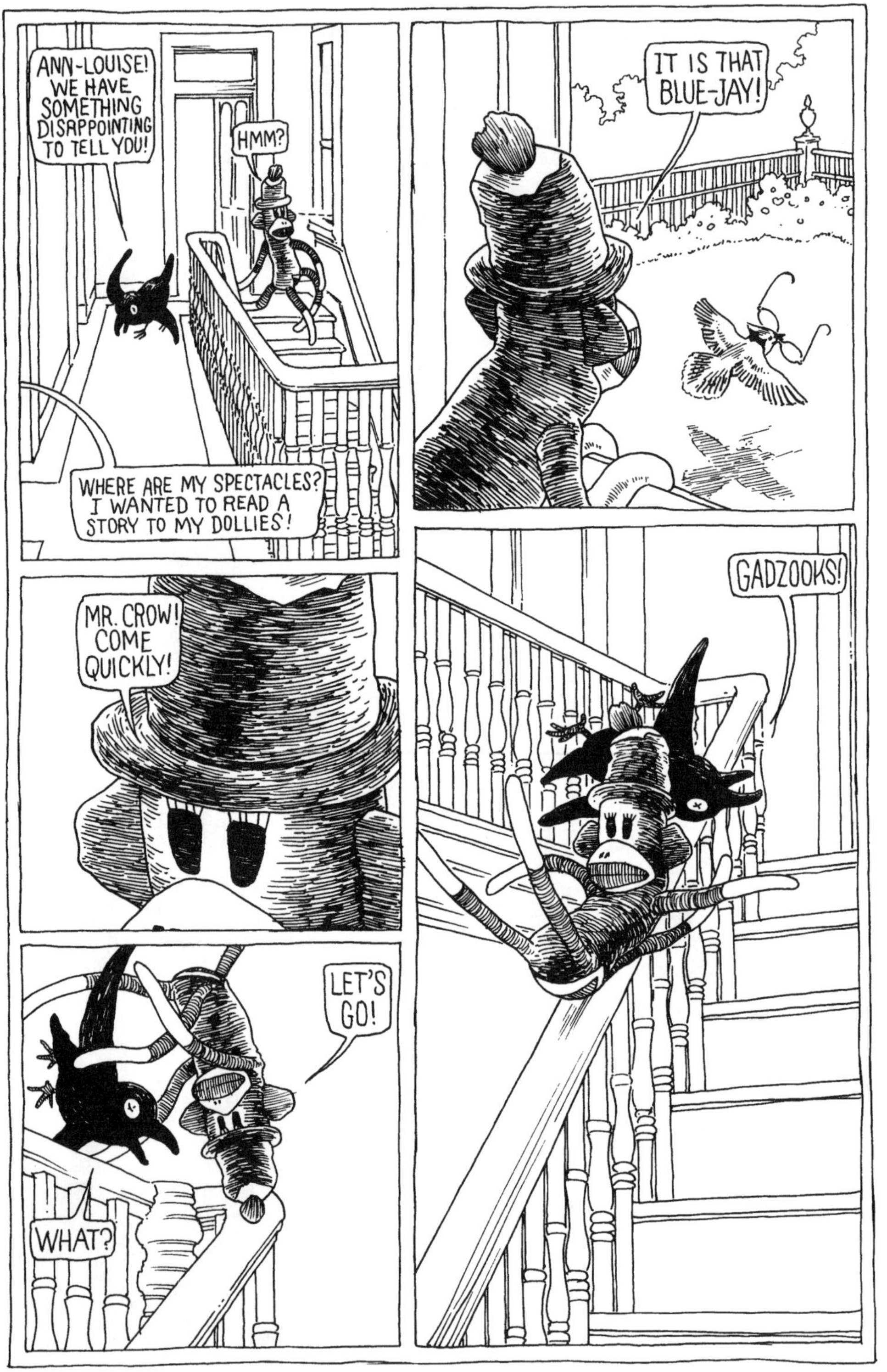
ANN-LOUISE! WE HAVE SOMETHING DISAPPOINTING TO TELL YOU!
HMM?
WHERE ARE MY SPECTACLES? I WANTED TO READ A STORY TO MY DOLLIES!
IT IS THAT BLUE-JAY!
MR. CROW! COME QUICKLY!
LET'S GO!
WHAT?
GADZOOKS!

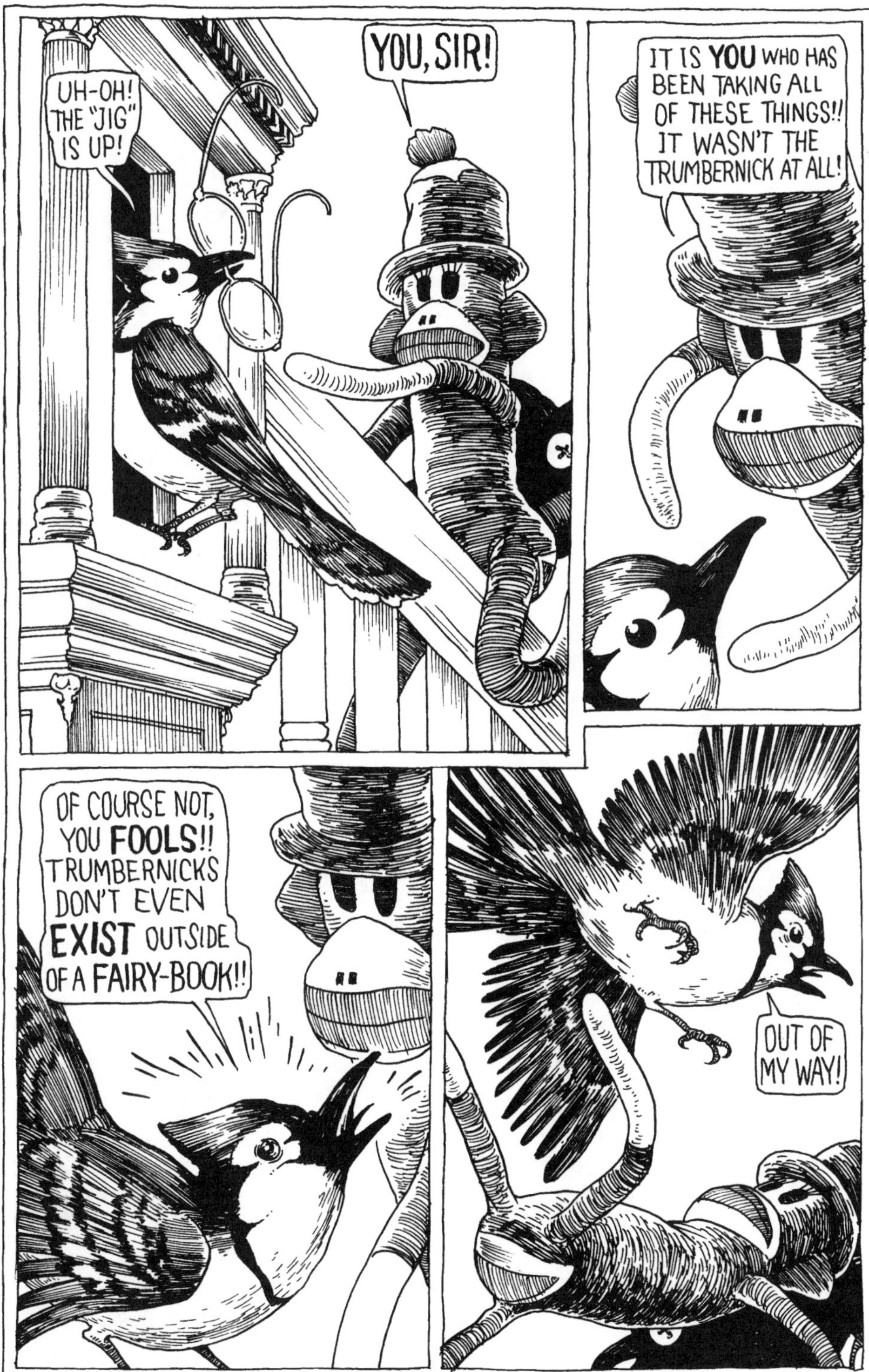
UH-OH! THE "JIG" IS UP!
YOU, SIR!
IT IS **YOU** WHO HAS BEEN TAKING ALL OF THESE THINGS!! IT WASN'T THE TRUMBERNICK AT ALL!
OF COURSE NOT, YOU **FOOLS**!! TRUMBERNICKS DON'T EVEN **EXIST** OUTSIDE OF A FAIRY-BOOK!!
OUT OF MY WAY!

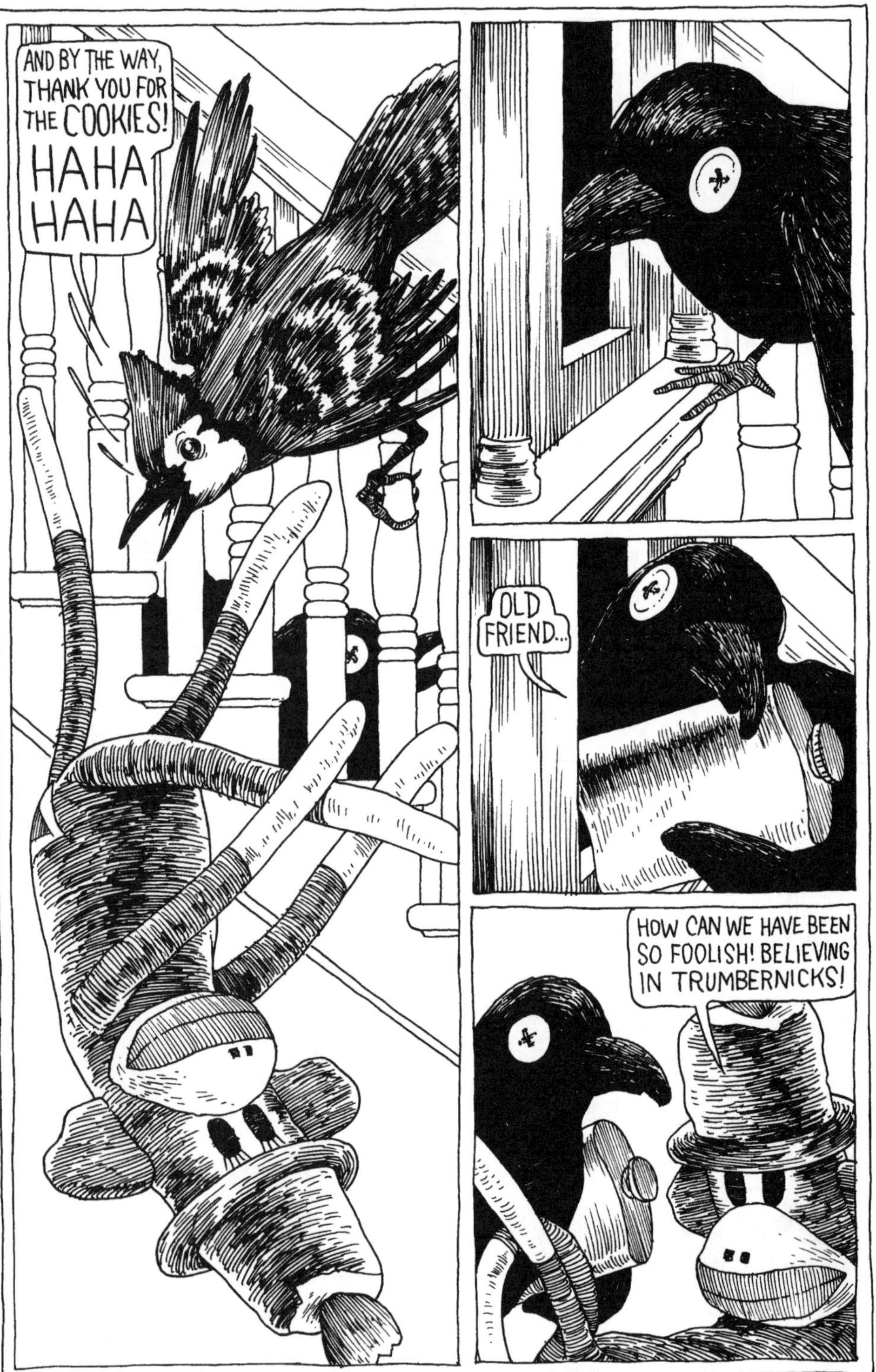
AND BY THE WAY, THANK YOU FOR THE COOKIES! HAHA HAHA
OLD FRIEND...
HOW CAN WE HAVE BEEN SO FOOLISH! BELIEVING IN TRUMBERNICKS!

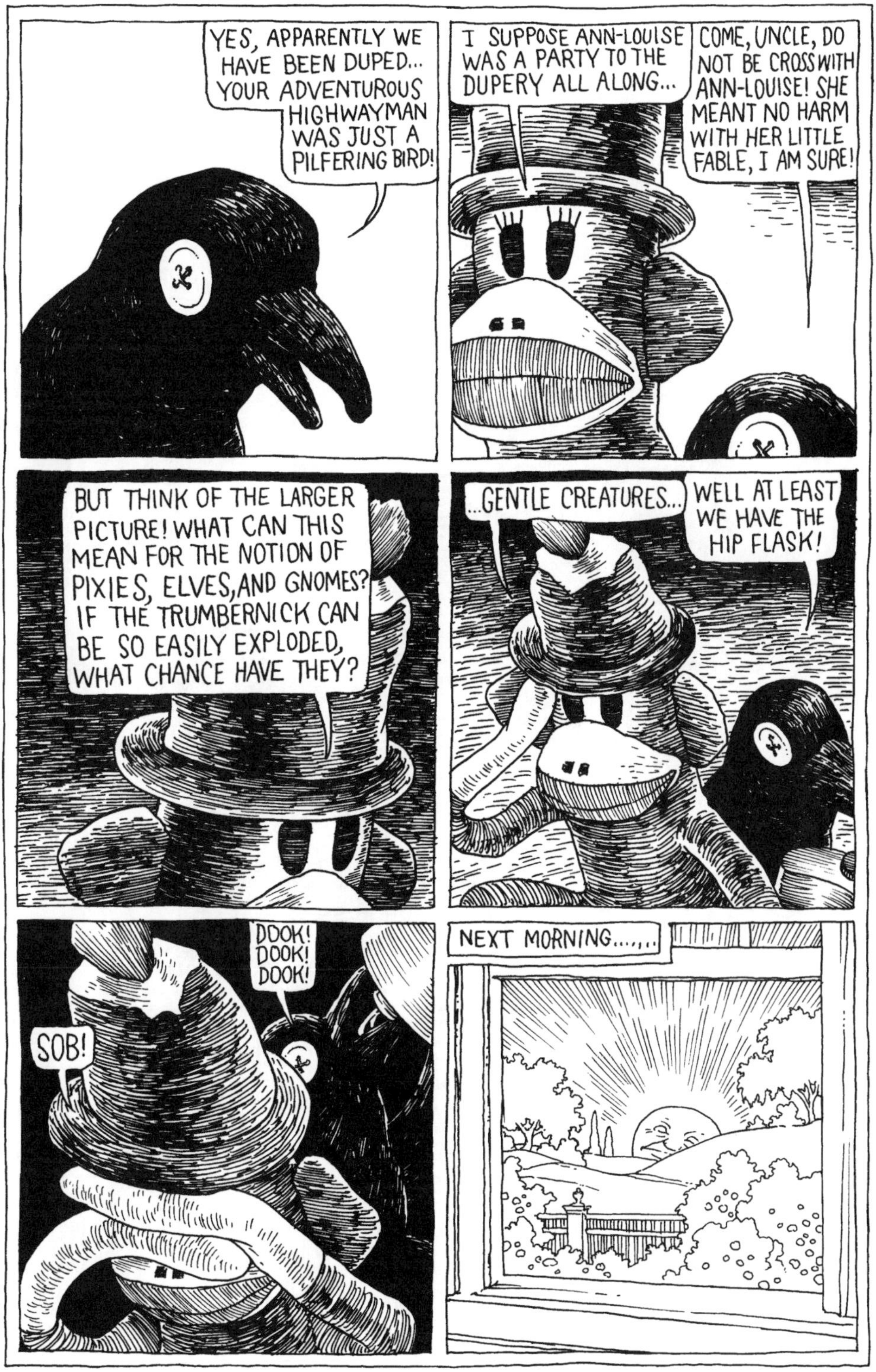
YES, APPARENTLY WE HAVE BEEN DUPED... YOUR ADVENTUROUS HIGHWAYMAN WAS JUST A PILFERING BIRD!
I SUPPOSE ANN-LOUISE WAS A PARTY TO THE DUPERY ALL ALONG...
COME, UNCLE, DO NOT BE CROSS WITH ANN-LOUISE! SHE MEANT NO HARM WITH HER LITTLE FABLE, I AM SURE!
BUT THINK OF THE LARGER PICTURE! WHAT CAN THIS MEAN FOR THE NOTION OF PIXIES, ELVES, AND GNOMES? IF THE TRUMBERNICK CAN BE SO EASILY EXPLODED, WHAT CHANCE HAVE THEY?
...GENTLE CREATURES...
WELL AT LEAST WE HAVE THE HIP FLASK!
DOOK! DOOK! DOOK!
SOB!
NEXT MORNING......

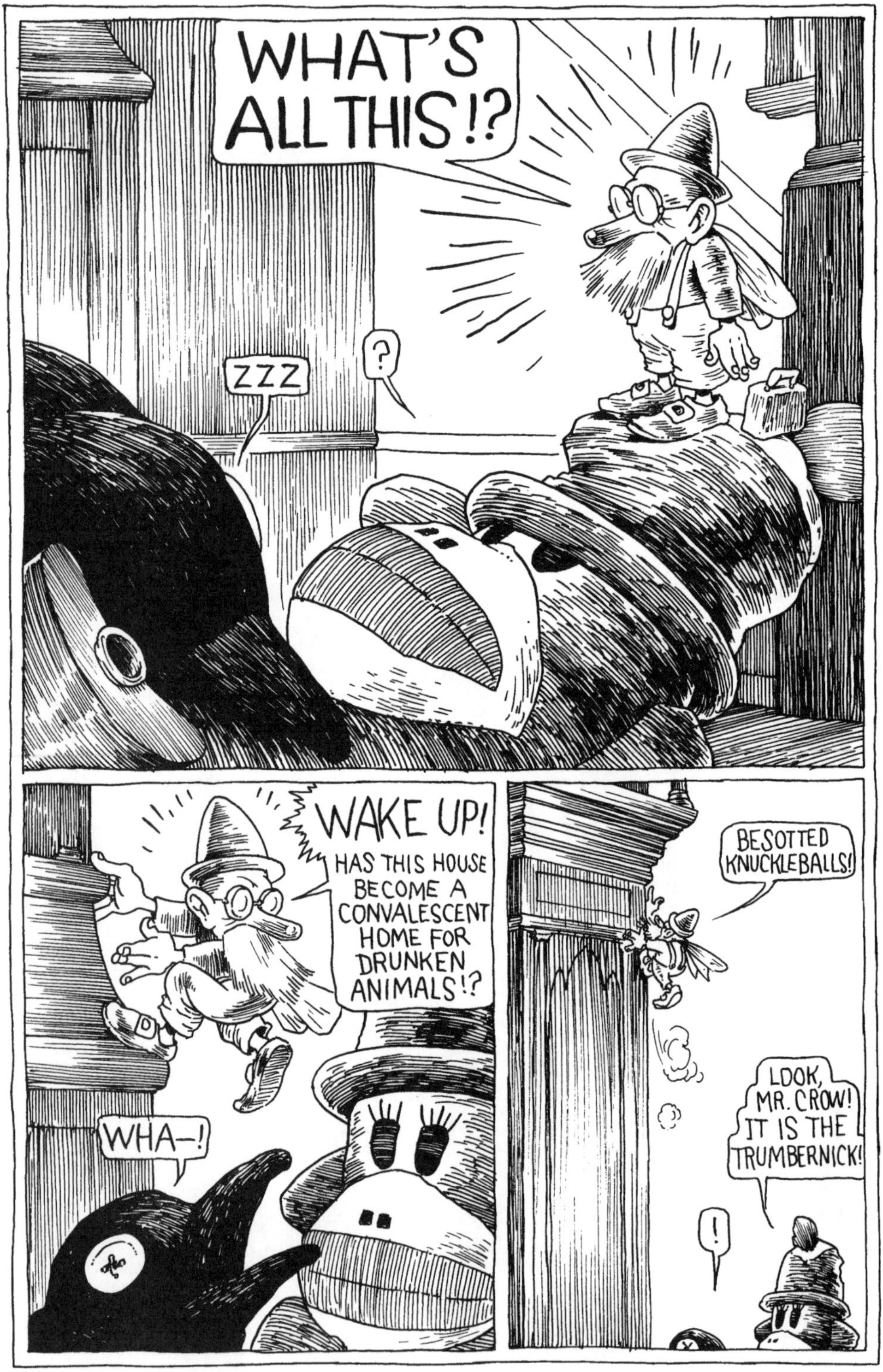
WHAT'S ALL THIS!?
ZZZ
?
WAKE UP!
HAS THIS HOUSE BECOME A CONVALESCENT HOME FOR DRUNKEN ANIMALS!?
WHA-!
BESOTTED KNUCKLEBALLS!
LOOK, MR. CROW! IT IS THE TRUMBERNICK!
!

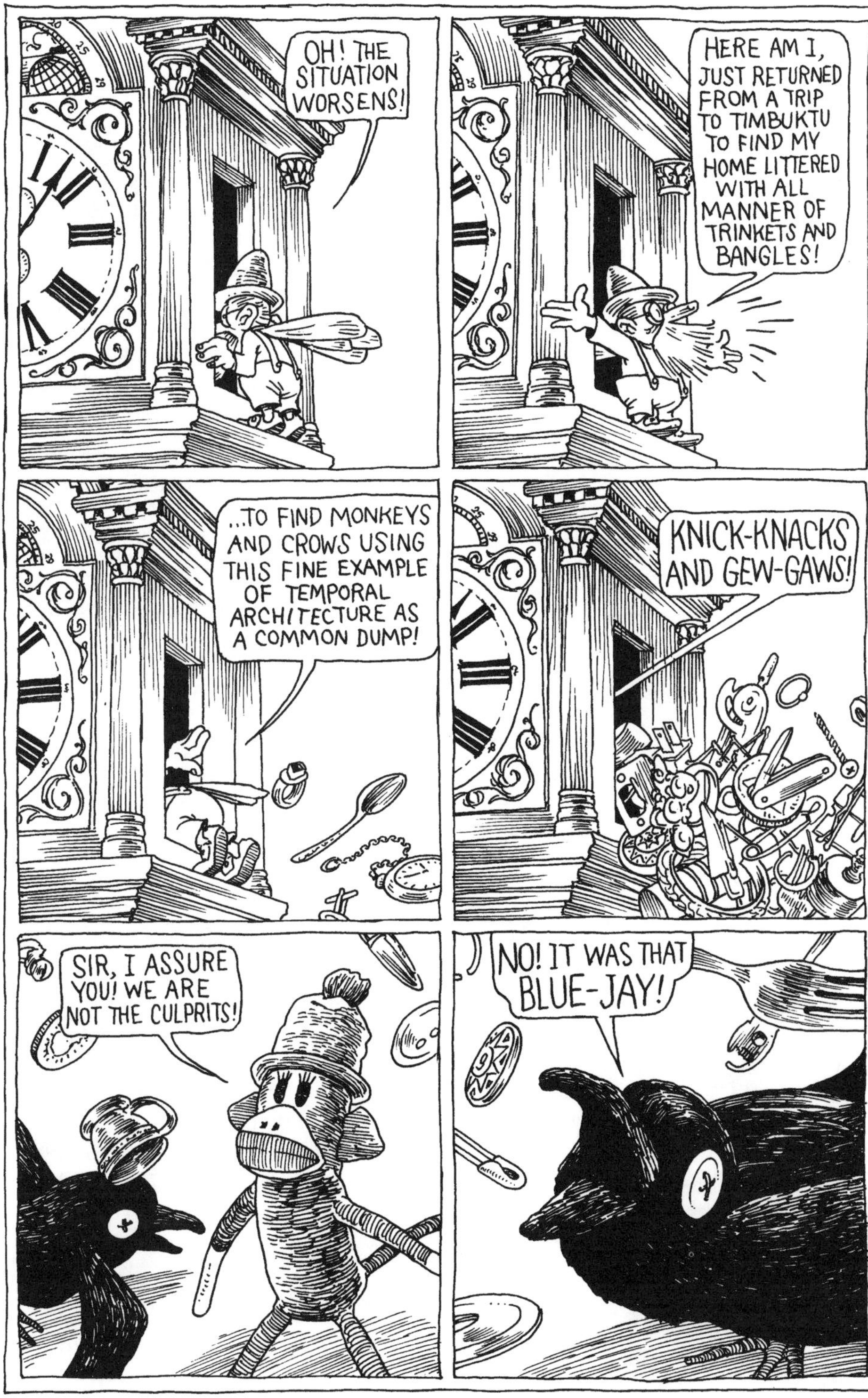
OH! THE SITUATION WORSENS!
HERE AM I, JUST RETURNED FROM A TRIP TO TIMBUKTU TO FIND MY HOME LITTERED WITH ALL MANNER OF TRINKETS AND BANGLES!
...TO FIND MONKEYS AND CROWS USING THIS FINE EXAMPLE OF TEMPORAL ARCHITECTURE AS A COMMON DUMP!
KNICK-KNACKS AND GEW-GAWS!
SIR, I ASSURE YOU! WE ARE NOT THE CULPRITS!
NO! IT WAS THAT BLUE-JAY!

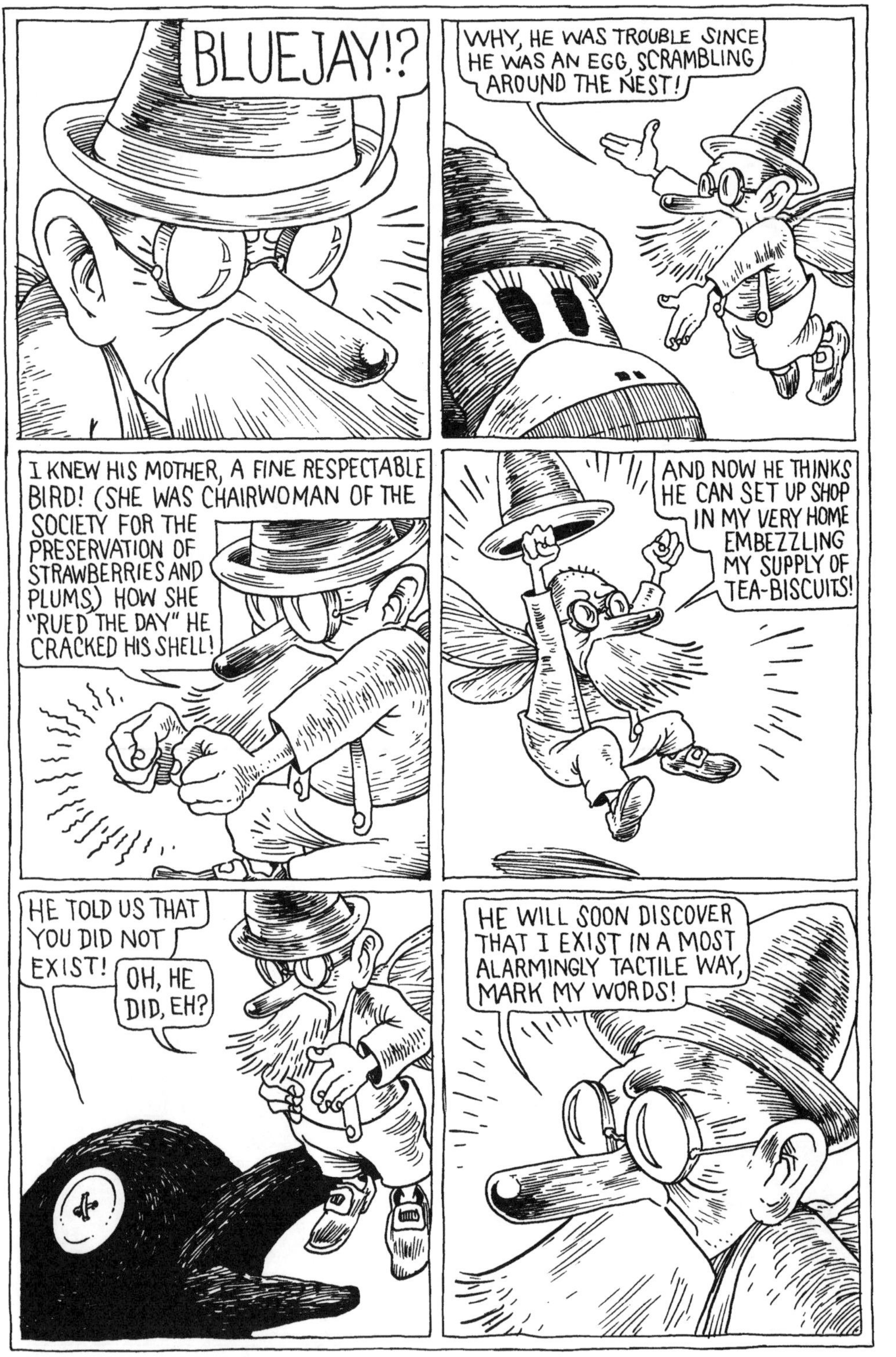
BLUEJAY!?
WHY, HE WAS TROUBLE SINCE HE WAS AN EGG, SCRAMBLING AROUND THE NEST!
I KNEW HIS MOTHER, A FINE RESPECTABLE BIRD! (SHE WAS CHAIRWOMAN OF THE SOCIETY FOR THE PRESERVATION OF STRAWBERRIES AND PLUMS) HOW SHE "RUED THE DAY" HE CRACKED HIS SHELL!
AND NOW HE THINKS HE CAN SET UP SHOP IN MY VERY HOME EMBEZZLING MY SUPPLY OF TEA-BISCUITS!
HE TOLD US THAT YOU DID NOT EXIST!
OH, HE DID, EH?
HE WILL SOON DISCOVER THAT I EXIST IN A MOST ALARMINGLY TACTILE WAY, MARK MY WORDS!

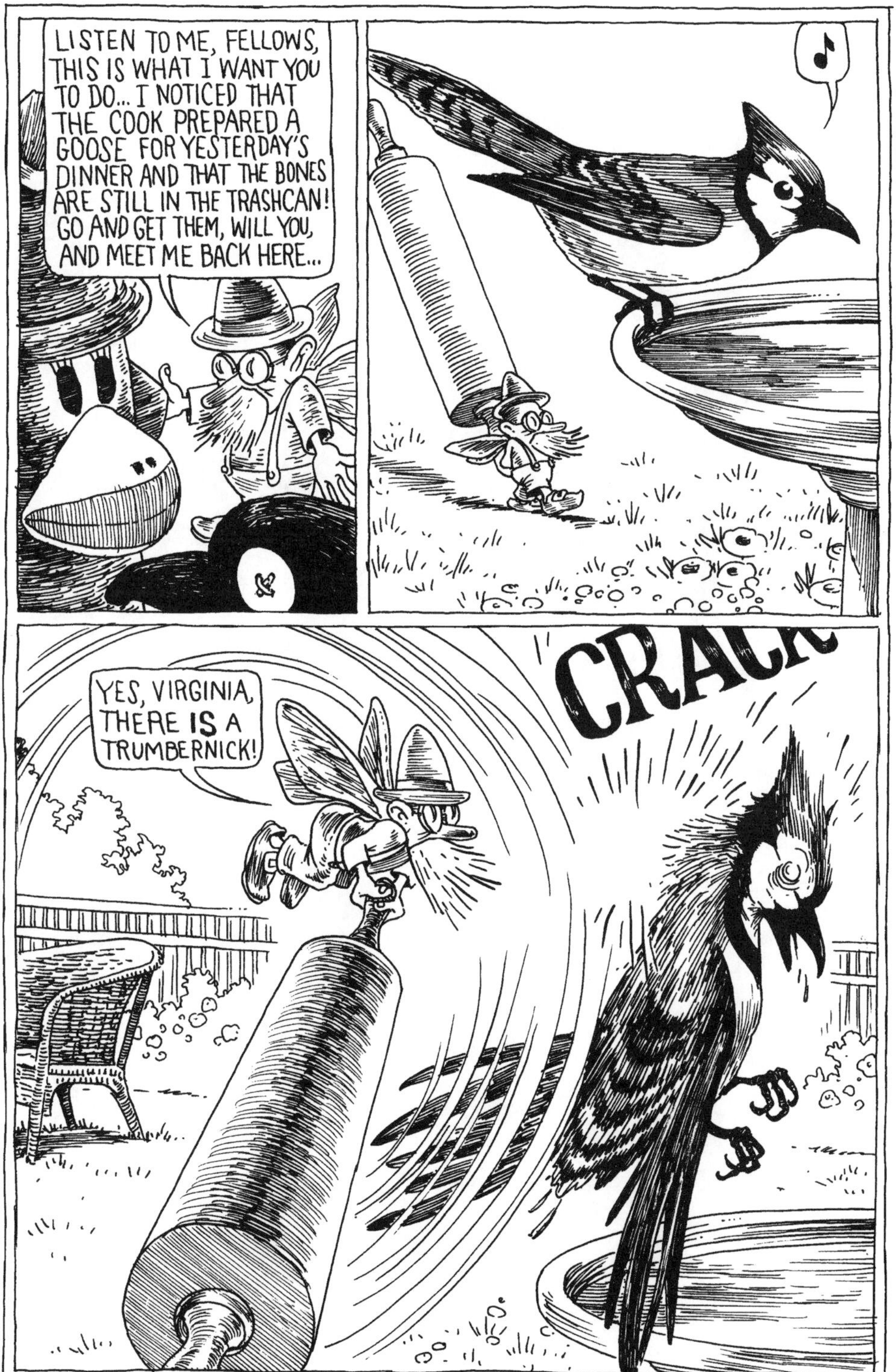
LISTEN TO ME, FELLOWS, THIS IS WHAT I WANT YOU TO DO... I NOTICED THAT THE COOK PREPARED A GOOSE FOR YESTERDAY'S DINNER AND THAT THE BONES ARE STILL IN THE TRASHCAN! GO AND GET THEM, WILL YOU, AND MEET ME BACK HERE...
♪
YES, VIRGINIA, THERE **IS** A TRUMBERNICK!
CRACK

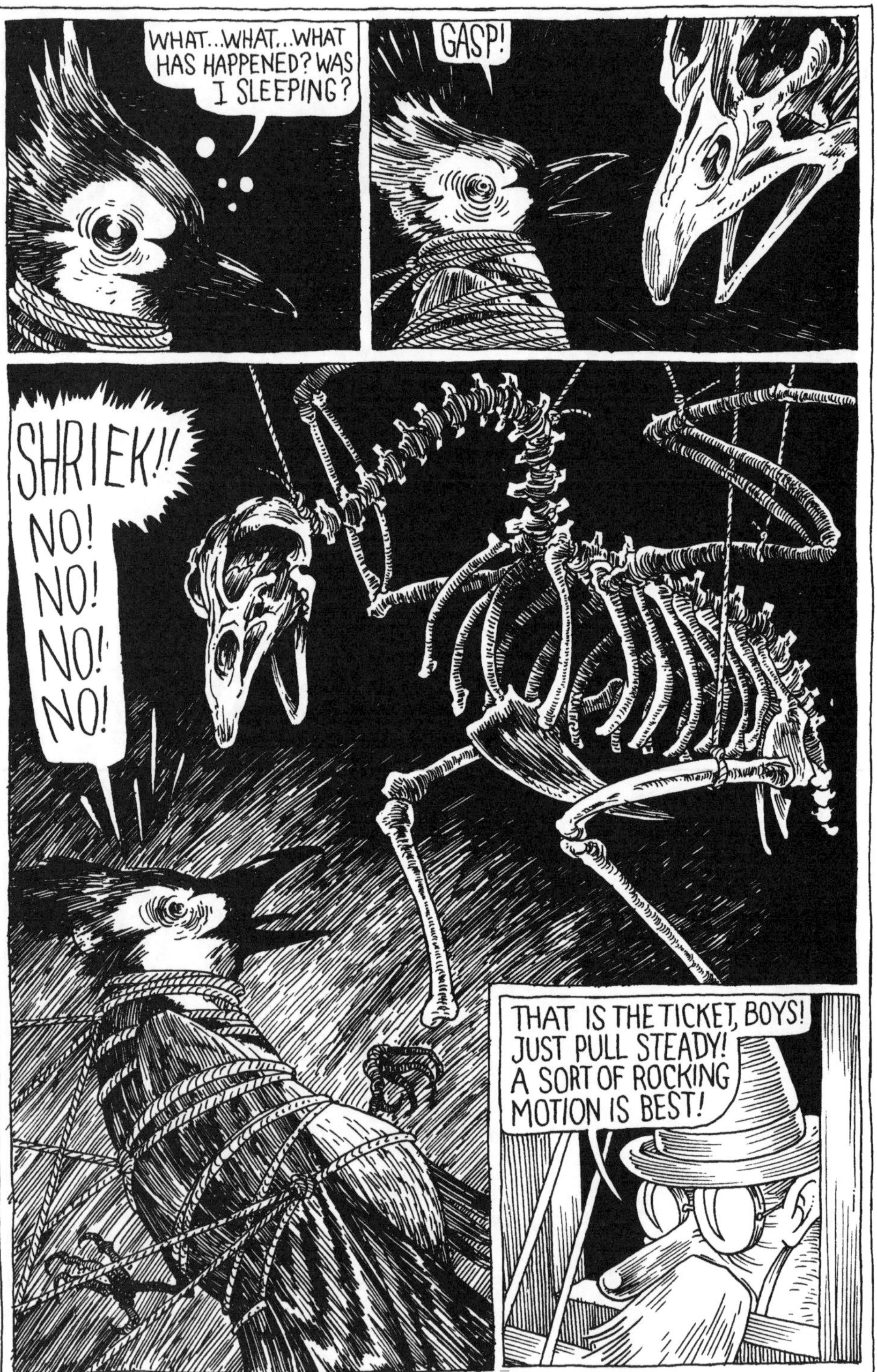
WHAT...WHAT...WHAT HAS HAPPENED? WAS I SLEEPING?
GASP!
SHRIEK!! NO! NO! NO! NO!
THAT IS THE TICKET, BOYS! JUST PULL STEADY! A SORT OF ROCKING MOTION IS BEST!

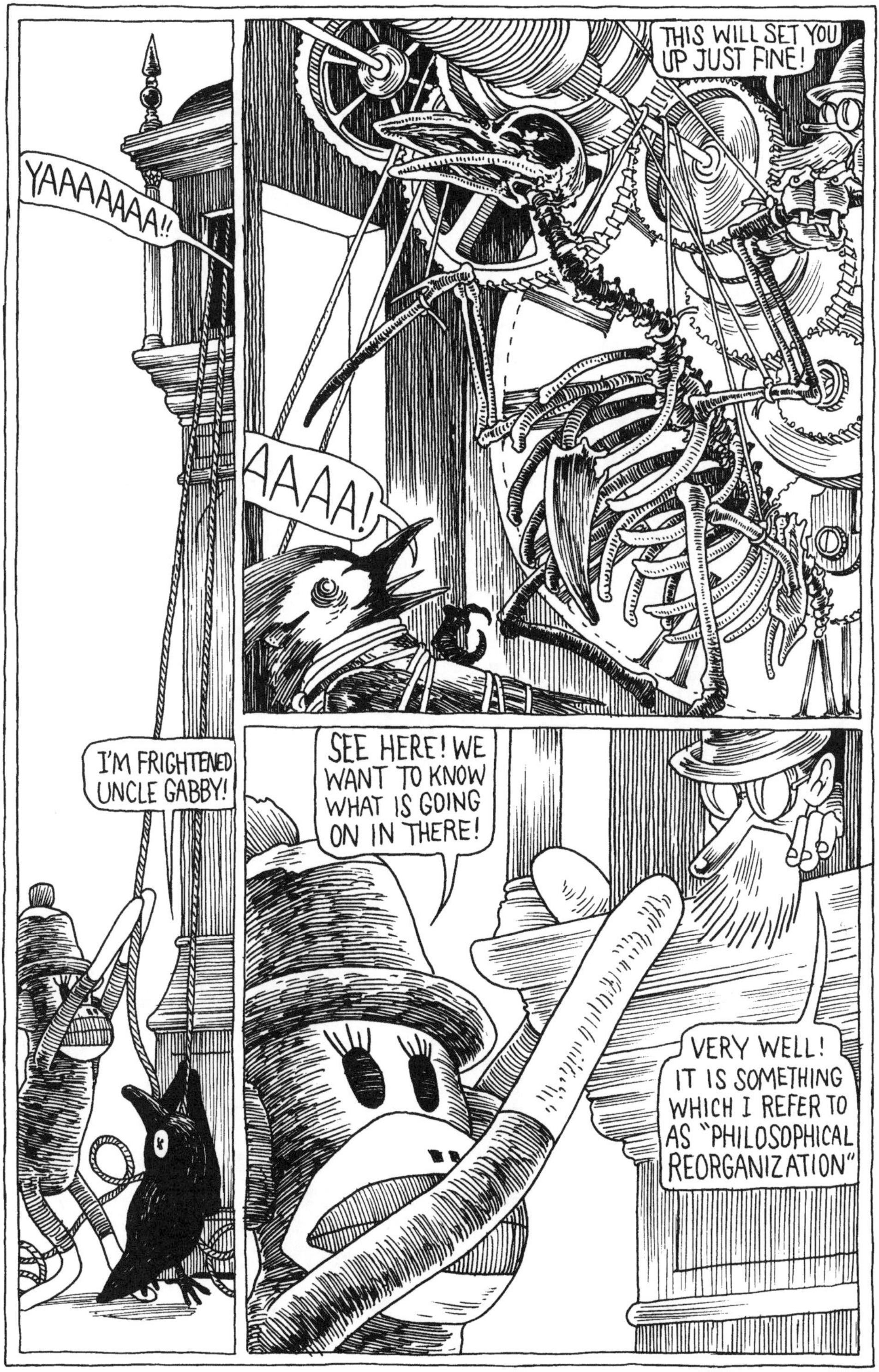
YAAAAAAA!!
I'M FRIGHTENED UNCLE GABBY!
THIS WILL SET YOU UP JUST FINE!
AAAA!
SEE HERE! WE WANT TO KNOW WHAT IS GOING ON IN THERE!
VERY WELL! IT IS SOMETHING WHICH I REFER TO AS "PHILOSOPHICAL REORGANIZATION"

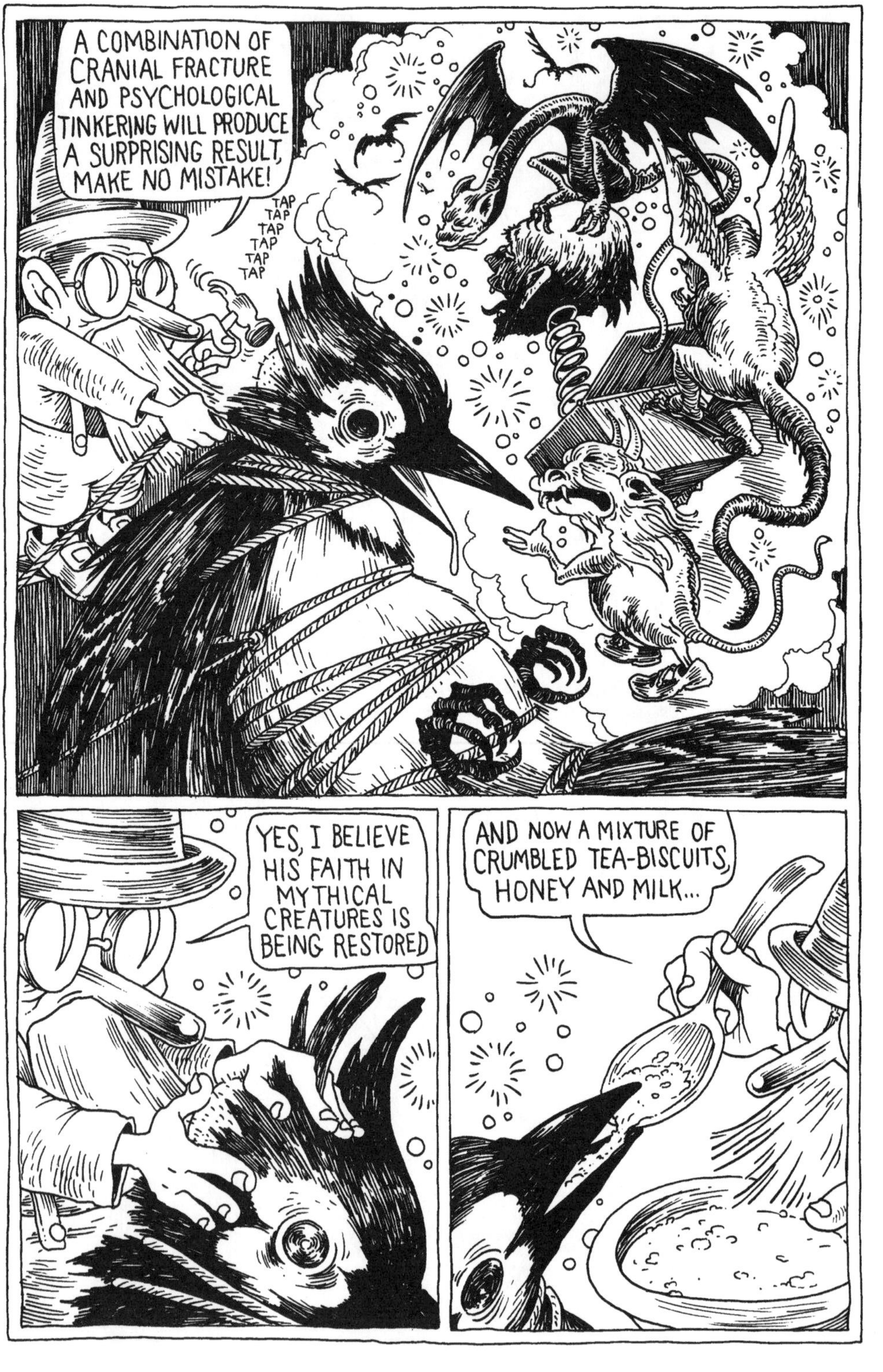
A COMBINATION OF CRANIAL FRACTURE AND PSYCHOLOGICAL TINKERING WILL PRODUCE A SURPRISING RESULT, MAKE NO MISTAKE!
TAP TAP TAP TAP TAP TAP
YES, I BELIEVE HIS FAITH IN MYTHICAL CREATURES IS BEING RESTORED
AND NOW A MIXTURE OF CRUMBLED TEA-BISCUITS, HONEY AND MILK...

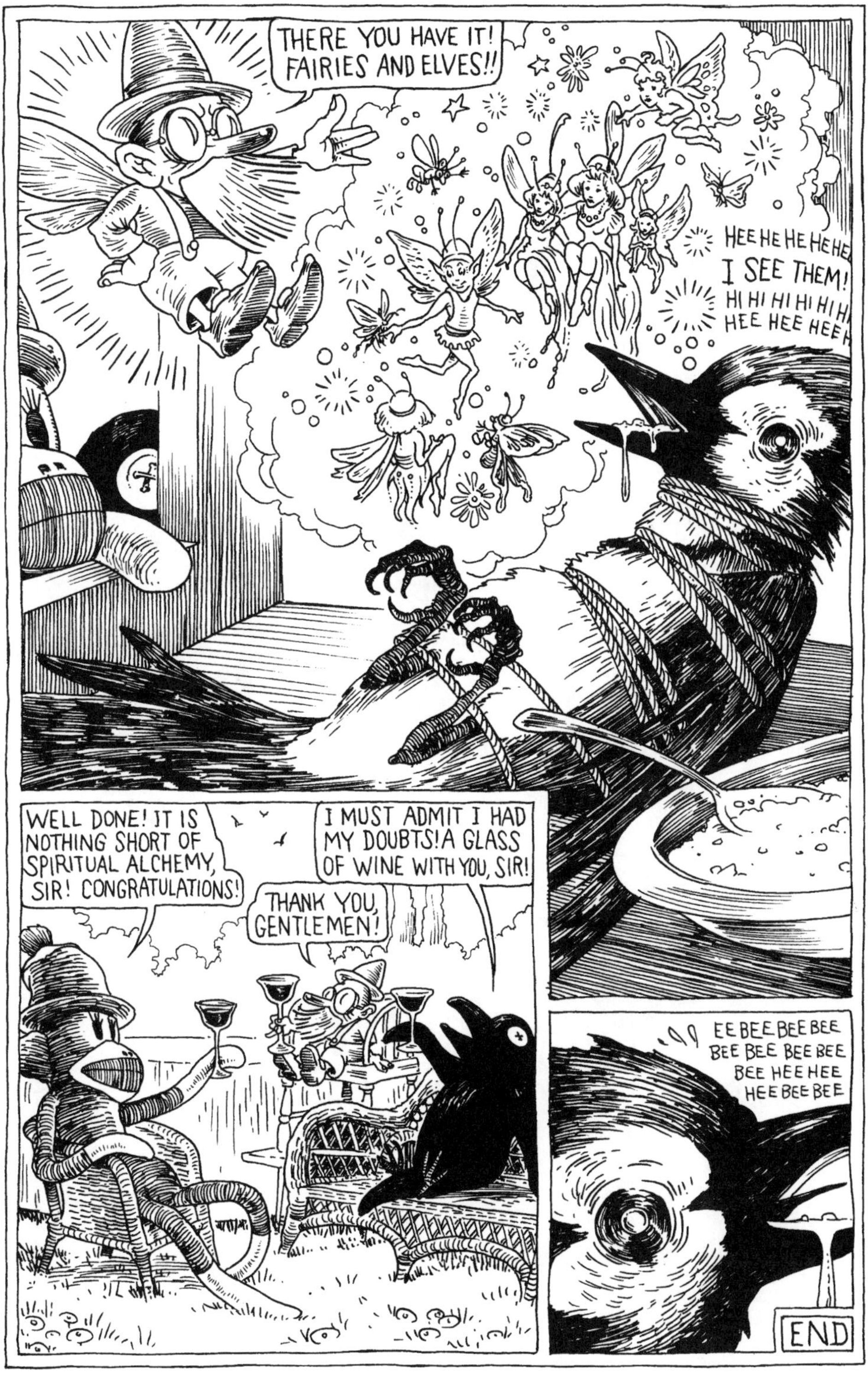
THERE YOU HAVE IT! FAIRIES AND ELVES!!
HEE HE HE HE HE
I SEE THEM!
HI HI HI HI HI
HEE HEE HEE
WELL DONE! IT IS NOTHING SHORT OF SPIRITUAL ALCHEMY, SIR! CONGRATULATIONS!
I MUST ADMIT I HAD MY DOUBTS! A GLASS OF WINE WITH YOU, SIR!
THANK YOU, GENTLEMEN!
EE BEE BEE BEE
BEE BEE BEE BEE
BEE HEE HEE
HEE BEE BEE
END

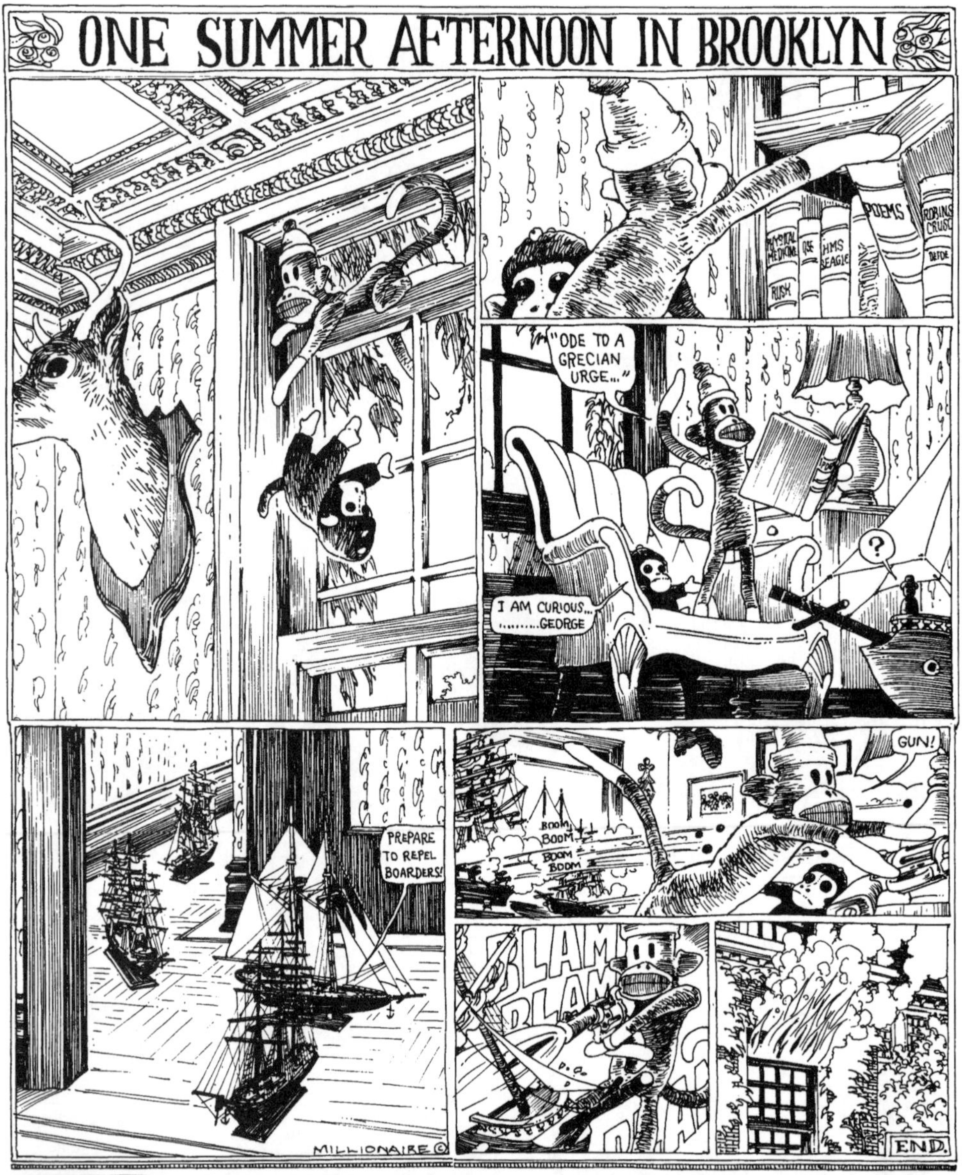
ONE SUMMER AFTERNOON IN BROOKLYN
PHYSICAL MEDICINE RUSH
POE
HMS BEAGLE
POEMS
ROBINSON CRUSOE DEFOE
"ODE TO A GRECIAN URGE..."
I AM CURIOUS... ....GEORGE
?
PREPARE TO REPEL BOARDERS!
MILLIONAIRE ©
GUN!
BOOM BOOM BOOM BOOM
BLAM BLAM
END.

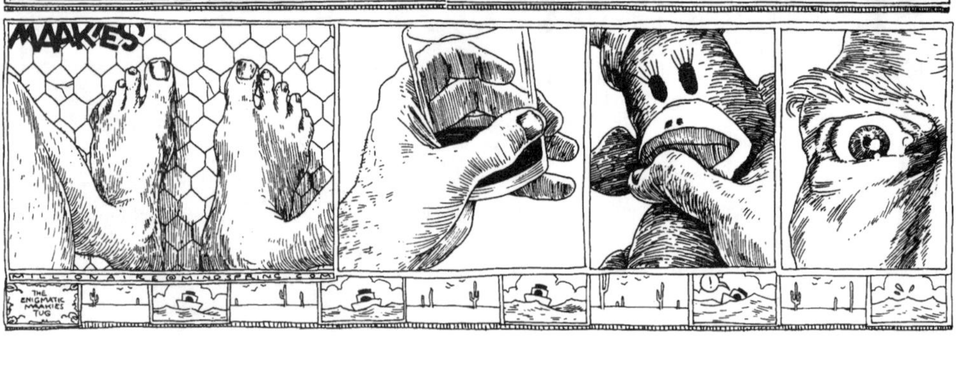
MAAKIES
MILLIONAIRE@MINDSPRING.COM
THE ENIGMATIC MAAKIES TUG
!

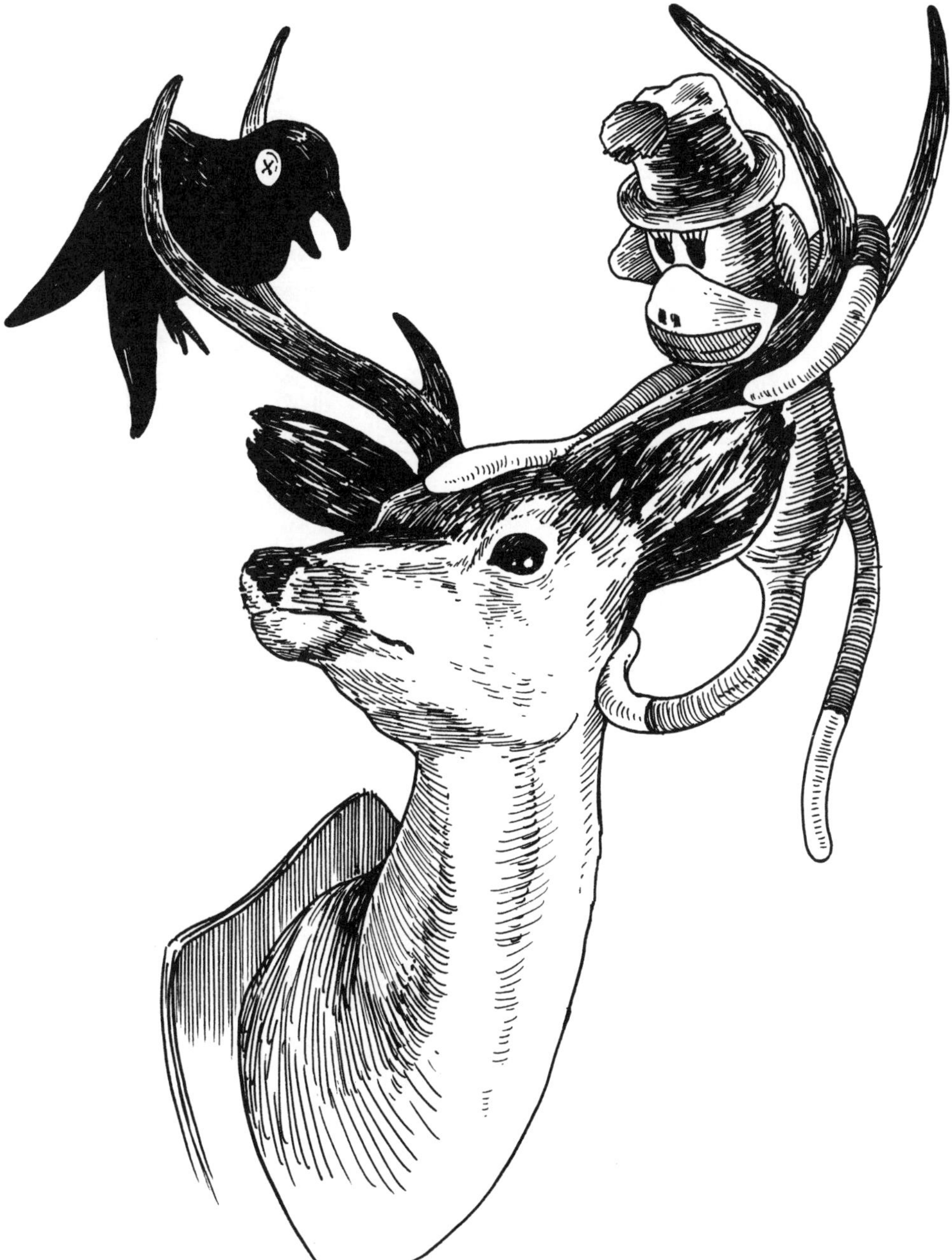

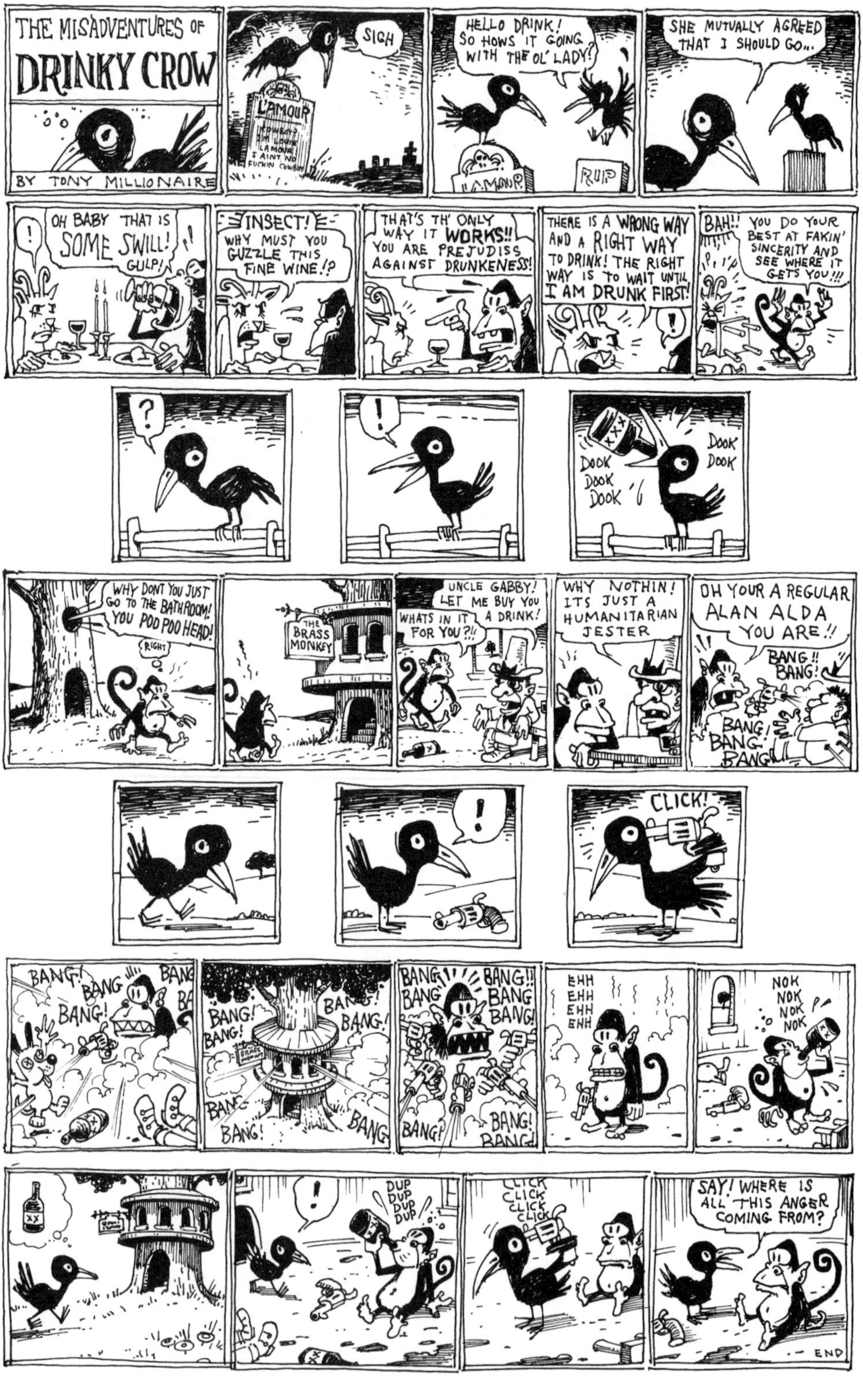

THE MISADVENTURES OF
DRINKY CROW
BY TONY MILLIONAIRE
SIGH
L'AMOUR
HELLO DRINK! SO HOWS IT GOING WITH THE OL' LADY?
RIP
SHE MUTUALLY AGREED THAT I SHOULD GO...
!
OH BABY THAT IS SOME SWILL!
GULP!
INSECT!
WHY MUST YOU GUZZLE THIS FINE WINE!?
THAT'S TH' ONLY WAY IT WORKS!! YOU ARE PREJUDISS AGAINST DRUNKENESS!
THERE IS A WRONG WAY AND A RIGHT WAY TO DRINK! THE RIGHT WAY IS TO WAIT UNTIL I AM DRUNK FIRST!
!
BAH!!
YOU DO YOUR BEST AT FAKIN' SINCERITY AND SEE WHERE IT GETS YOU!!!
?
!
DOOK DOOK DOOK
DOOK DOOK
WHY DONT YOU JUST GO TO THE BATHROOM! YOU POO POO HEAD!
RIGHT
THE BRASS MONKEY
UNCLE GABBY! LET ME BUY YOU A DRINK!
WHATS IN IT FOR YOU?!!
WHY NOTHIN! ITS JUST A HUMANITARIAN JESTER
OH YOUR A REGULAR ALAN ALDA YOU ARE!!
BANG!! BANG!
BANG! BANG! BANG
!
CLICK!
BANG! BANG BANG!
BANG! BANG! BANG! BANG! BANG BANG!
BANG! BANG
BANG!! BANG BANG!
BANG! BANG!
EHH EHH EHH EHH
NOK NOK NOK NOK
!
DUP DUP DUP DUP
CLICK CLICK CLICK CLICK
SAY! WHERE IS ALL THIS ANGER COMING FROM?
END

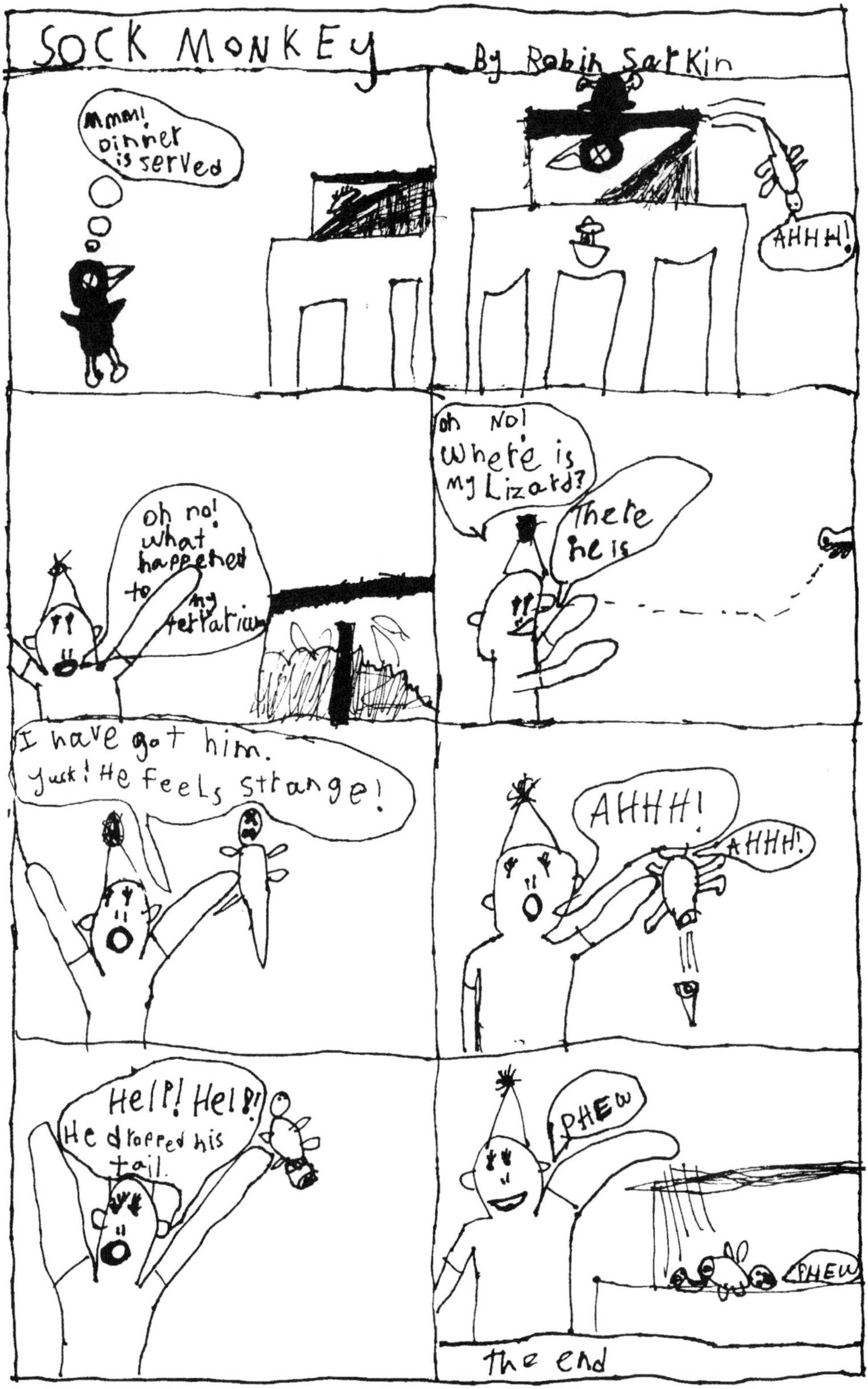
SOCK MONKEY
By Robin Sarkin
Mmm! Dinner is served
AHHH!
Oh no! what happened to my terrarium
Oh No! Where is my Lizard?
There he is
I have got him. Yuck! He feels strange!
AHHH!
AHHH!
Help! Help! He dropped his tail.
PHEW
PHEW
the end

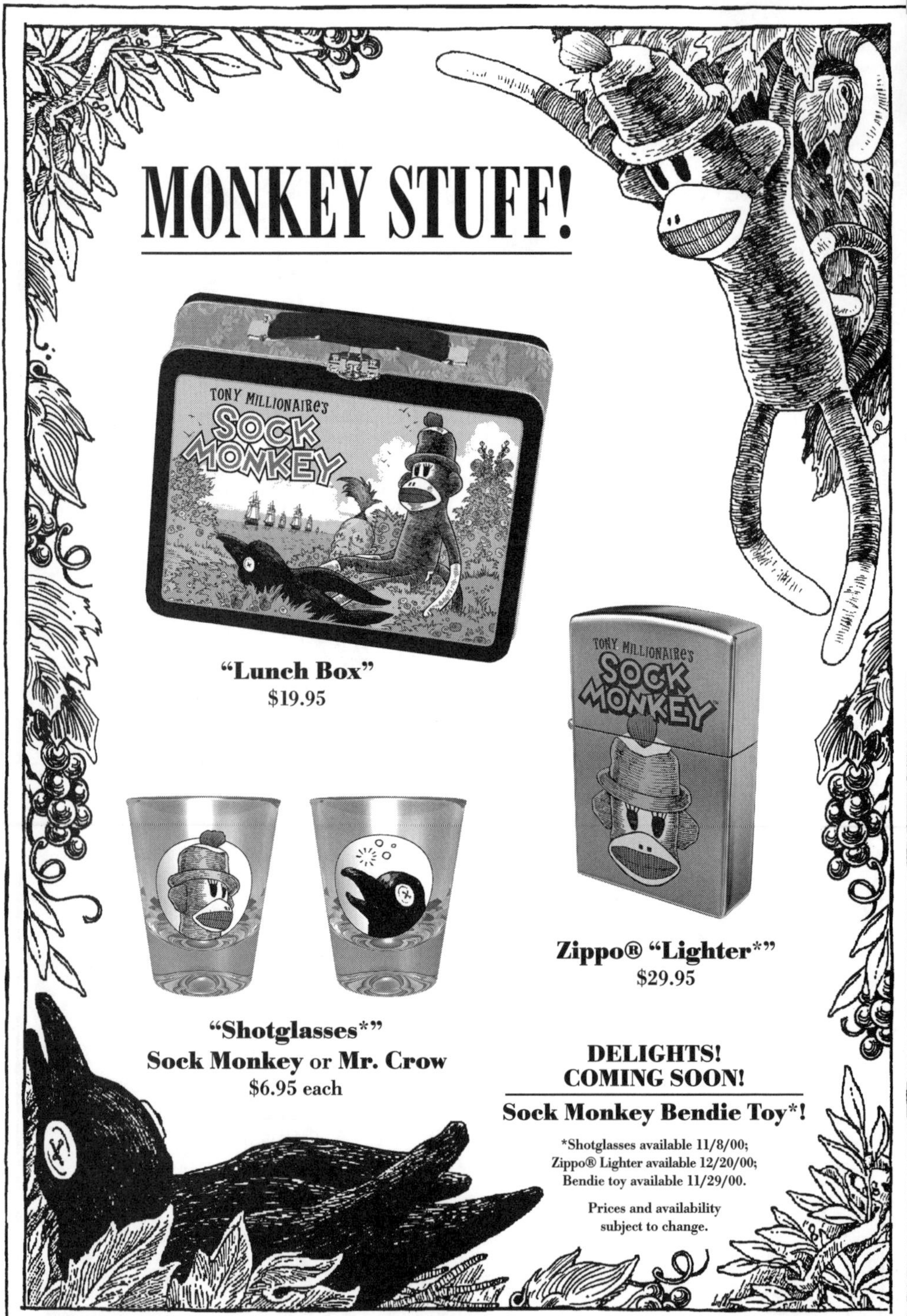
MONKEY STUFF!
TONY MILLIONAIRE's
SOCK MONKEY
"Lunch Box"
$19.95
TONY MILLIONAIRE's
SOCK MONKEY
Zippo® "Lighter*"
$29.95
"Shotglasses*"
Sock Monkey or Mr. Crow
$6.95 each
DELIGHTS!
COMING SOON!
Sock Monkey Bendie Toy*!
*Shotglasses available 11/8/00;
Zippo® Lighter available 12/20/00;
Bendie toy available 11/29/00.
Prices and availability
subject to change.